ARCHIPENKO

International Visionary

Edited by
Donald H. Karshan

Preface by S. Dillon Ripley
Foreword by David W. Scott
Essay by Guy Habasque

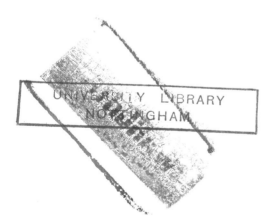
Published for the
National Collection of Fine Arts
by Smithsonian Institution Press
City of Washington
1969

Distribution in the United States and Canada by
Random House, Inc.
American Standard Book Number 87474-080-0

Distribution in the United Kingdom and Europe by
David & Charles (Publishers), Ltd., South Devon House, Newton Abbot, Devon, England
British Standard Book Number 7153-9570-X

Library of Congress Catalogue Card Number: 71-77509

First printing 1969

Designed and produced by Chanticleer Press, Inc.
Printed by Amilcare Pizzi, S. p. A., Milan, Italy

Contents

Preface

James Smithson founded the Smithsonian Institution in 1846 for "the increase and diffusion of knowledge among men." Since then the Smithsonian has become the largest complex of museums in the world. One of its many functions in the scientific world community is that of major publisher and distributor of technical literature.

"The man of science has no country; the world is his country, all men his countryman," Smithson said, and this is also true for the man of arts. Esthetic needs are universal, as are the most refined metaphors of the artist. There are esthetic as well as scientific inventions.

Alexander Archipenko was an artist of this international scope, and his inventions were among the most pivotal in modern sculpture. Although America was privileged with this great artist's presence, he truly belongs to the world.

The Smithsonian Institution is pleased to circulate the Archipenko Retrospective Exhibition to many nations, and to publish, in several languages, this book on his life and works. In so doing, the Smithsonian pursues the task set forth by its great founder.

S. Dillon Ripley
Secretary
Smithsonian Institution

Foreword

When Archipenko came to America at the age of thirty-six, he had already achieved fame as a sculptor associated with art movements underway in France, Germany and Italy. Five years later, in 1928, he became a naturalized citizen of the United States, where he lived for the remaining forty-one years of his life. His artistic production was unceasing. His teaching, which began in Europe, continued in America and encompassed cities from coast to coast. He also continued his writings, culminating in his "Polychrome Manifesto" of 1959, which is published in this catalogue. When he died in 1964 at the age of seventy-six, his American works numbered over 750 pieces. His influence had extended over American and European artists of two generations, and is still being felt today.

In the summer of 1968, when the National Collection of Fine Arts held the first one-man exhibition in its new building and inaugurated its sculpture gallery, it presented the Archipenko Memorial Retrospective. We were delighted, therefore, when Mrs. Archipenko generously offered to lend a substantial portion of her collection to the National Collection of Fine Arts for an overseas tour. Our International Art Program, under the direction of Miss Lois A. Bingham, promptly organized a tour which includes many of the major museums in Europe.

The range of Archipenko's work created in America and the continuous flow of ideas which this work reflects have their origins in his early experiences and exposure to traditions in the Europe of his formative years. Many of the important works of this early period are included in the European touring exhibition to provide the opportunity for the deepest appreciation of Archipenko's total creativity.

David W. Scott, Director
National Collection of Fine Arts
Smithsonian Institution

Introduction

During the fifty-six years since the catalogue of Archipenko's first one-man exhibition in 1912, much diverse literature on the artist has appeared in many nations and languages. Although nearly all were monographs of modest size, this voluminous documentation is witness to the artist's enormous international standing, his prodigous output and his own extensive travels and exhibition schedules. The most ambitious of these publications were Hans Hildebrandt's monograph in 1923 and the 1967 catalogue of the Memorial Retrospective organized by the University of California at Los Angeles with an introduction by Frederick Wight. By far the most informative effort has been the sculptor's own, *Archipenko: Fifty Creative Years,* profusely illustrated with the artist's sculpture through 1959 and published privately in a limited edition.

The editor has combined and amplified elements from these publications by reproducing the artist's work in several mediums, giving copious extracts from his writings, many of them unpublished, and adding several selected essays on his art. In addition to an extensive biographical chronology, the artist's life and art are, for the first time, concurrently documented through photographs, newspaper clippings, catalogues, handwritten items, and other memorabilia from the Estate Collection. All of this material is integrated with the reproductions of sculpture, paintings, drawings and prints, presented in chronological order and divided, for convenience, into four sections, corresponding to the Russian, French, German, and American periods of the artist's career. The black and white illustrations have been printed in hand-fed gravure in an attempt to capture refinements in the works themselves and the wealth of detail in the memorabilia. Color printing has been used to present as faithfully as possible Archipenko's contributions to polychrome sculpture and what he termed "Sculpto-Peintures." What is perhaps Archipenko's most important writing, his "Polychrome Manifesto" of 1959, is offered in its entirety. Although published in that year, the essay most likely was conceived many years earlier. Dates of the artist's writings, which Archipenko often refined, revised and even translated, are therefore difficult to establish and are only indicated when firmly known.

In reviewing the many introductions to former catalogues of Archipenko exhibitions, particularly those before he left for America, the writings of Guillaume Apollinaire struck this editor as combining eloquence of interpretation with unique insights into the artist's awareness of ancient and primitive art. (Archipenko had said about his youthful years in Paris that his "real school" was the Louvre.) Therefore, essays by Apollinaire and Guy Habasque were selected for republication as part of a manifold introduction. Guy Habasque, the French art historian, came to know the sculptor and his work during meetings in Europe and America in the late 1950s. The illustrated section concludes with a comment by Madame Archipenko on the Estate Collection and its responsibilities. The editor sifted hundreds of photographs and documents in an attempt to create a pictorial representation of some of the salient events in the artist's life. The discovery of several views of the artist at work was particularly fortunate; such examples are juxtaposed with close-up photographs of the completed sculpture. Caricatures ridiculing Archipenko's art reproduced in these pages poignantly reveal the condemnation endured by the sculptor over the years.

Archipenko's works reproduced in this volume were selected from those included in the retrospective exhibition organized by the Smithsonian Institution's International Art Program for a tour of several nations in 1969 through 1971. That exhibition was, in turn, assembled exclusively from the Estate Collection. Catalogues raisonnés of Archipenko's sculpture and graphic art, now under preparation by this editor, will present the entire range of Archipenko's extraordinary creative activity.

The text of this volume has been translated for English, French, and German editions—the first such effort with an Archipenko publication since the Hildebrandt monograph nearly a half century ago. The resultant international readership befits an artist whose sculptural statements were truly international in their vision.

Finally, I should like to express my appreciation to Miss Lois A. Bingham, Chief of the International Art Program, and to its staff which has helped immeasurably in the creation of this volume. Particular thanks are extended to Miss Margaret Cogswell, Deputy Chief of the International Art Program, whose counsel during our discussions of the catalogue contributed to its final form and to Mrs. Esther Harmon, Research Assistant, who helped in the difficult task of collating copy and captions.

Donald H. Karshan
New York
November 1968

Alexander Archipenko

by Guillaume Apollinaire (1912)

It is creative powers that give the art of Archipenko its direction. Even in the first compositions which this young Russian sculptor exhibited in Paris, there were to be found changes in direction, sudden and yet tender changes which (if Archipenko moves forward farther as he has gone to date) one could term a shifting of gears—to borrow an expression from the new language born of industry.

Archipenko builds realities. His art approaches absolute sculpture closer and closer, a sculpture which will one day amalgamate with absolute painting and absolute architecture, an art beyond all style, beyond all techniques and auxiliary means.

Archipenko has in him the powers which are needed in order to convert into reality this goal of inward plastic unity.

The sole ones, among all artists, that have striven earnestly toward this goal are our new painters: Picasso, Derain, Braque, Delaunay. It has not occurred to sculptors, save perhaps to the gifted Rude, who is the greatest among them. The others—Carpeaux, Rodin the great patriarch in the art field, Schnegg, Despiau—have preserved the forming power of light, have freed forms, have let them play and take on color, have subjected them to the sensual sensitivity of the eye.

On the other hand, Nadelmann sought a way, even though only timidly, and surpassed the Greeks and the Egyptians in *musical* constructions. He tried to bring plastic art back closer to architecture (scientific cubism). This is the way the paths were opened for an art which unites the great charm of sensually beautiful surfaces to inner plastic tectonics.

Archipenko's bold constructions softly but firmly proclaim the unheard-of possibilitie of this new art.

Colors and lights slip flowingly over the forms become man and seem to permeate t em. The vaultings, the complementary forms, the differentiation of the surfaces, depressions and elevatioi s, which are never sharply delimited, grow into living stone to which an impassioned blow of the chisel has lent sculptural expression.

One should look at this *Salome,* making her pressing desires almost gruesomely plain; this *Bathing Woman* which seems ever changing, ever new; this *Repose* or the *Sitting Woman,* which proclaim a fragment of life—look, and be still.

Hitherto sculpture has limited itself almost exclusively to being *melody.* In Archipenko's art, of which the first chords respond here, it seems to grow into a great harmony. The power of the creator shapes work and medium and expression; what drives it, and what his works give voice to, is the highly gifted, delicately organized personality of the artist, and what he seeks is realism. He works passionately upon the incorporation of his ideal: "Reality."

(Introduction to Archipenko's first one-man exhibition, Folkwang Museum, Hagen, Germany, December 1912. Translated by H. Bartlett Wells)

Alexander Archipenko

by Guillaume Apollinaire (1914)

In sculpture Archipenko seeks first and foremost purity of forms. He strives to discover and to fashion those which are abstract, symbolic, and most novel.

One observes in his art a complete adaptation of tradition. Superficial spirits may overlook this, but it is clear to those who wish to discern it.

The novelty of Archipenko's temperament appears at first glance to prohibit one's crediting an influence through the art of earlier centuries. But he has drawn from it everything that he could; he is convinced that he can boldly transcend it.

Stupidity and ignorance will always allege that the tango and the bunny-hug are less esthetic than traditional dances, even though they do embody in themselves the whole tradition they oppose.

Archipenko has been nourished by the best of what tradition offers. And the charm of his works is due to inward order, which shows itself without his seeming to seek it and which constitutes the skeleton of his curious figures in the completely renewed exquisite distinction of their forms.

If one were to wish to sum up his art in a concrete formula, I should like to see it represented by one of those splendidly tattooed queens from the Marquesas Islands, their skins bleached almost to European tints ... a queen dancing before the altar of the sea-god Atoua in a boisterous cancan, learned, perhaps, from some French sailor or a convict escaped from New Caledonia.

In the solemn character of Archipenko's art one feels the religious influence in the development of his temperament. Naive, pious pictures were, one may suppose, a joy to his childish eyes, which lit up and opened wide in astonishment. I should not be surprised if in his childhood he made little altars of soap-boxes and blue lace-paper and set upon them a gilt plaster figure of the Holy Virgin or a Byzantine icon, with tiny wax tapers on silvered candlesticks set round about.

As with all mystics, his senses awoke early. Did this occur at so early a time as this, so that there then took place this combination of these two strands, which one may call the father and the mother of his art?

He grasped the need of belonging above all to his own time, and to catch up in his art the life of the present.

His work shows signs that he was early attracted by the sacred nakedness of oriental mythological art. Greek sculpture instructed him. But the purer and more mystical sculpture of Egypt revealed plastic art and style to him and influenced him most strongly.

A hieroglyphic papyrus of Teutamoin allured him by reason of its erotic, symbolical representation of heaven and earth. The graven images of the priestesses, the gods scantily clad in leopard pelts, the figures of the Athlophoroi [prize-bearers] of Berenice Euergetes and the Canephoroi [basket-bearers] of Arsinoe Philadelpha or of Arsinoe Philopator, the religious dancers on the graves of Thebes or of Beni-Hanan, fructified his fancy. Rapidly passing visions moved him mightily.

He took in with astonishment the barbaric features of the idols of African tribes upon the bas-reliefs of the Speos of Beit-Qualli, and the extraordinary gestures of the Negro prisoners of war represented upon the great Speos at Istanbul passionately inspired him.

He pursued his research further and made the acquaintance of Chinese art. The Sakyamuni of the India House Museum brought him to recognize the superficiality of Greek art.

The representations of the birth of Buddha, of the bamboo garden of Kiä-lan-Hio, and of the cycle of metamorphoses excited his pious soul. Now for the first time he felt his true vocation and commenced lovingly to shape human forms. He studied with shrewdness the procedures of the modern masters whose temperament seemed most closely related to his own. The Florentine period with its sensuality took effect upon him, and da Vinci, Botticelli, and Giovanni da Bologna opened to him bit by bit the secrets of their art. Jean Goujon influenced him too, as did French sensuality of the eighteenth century in Falconet and Clodion. From these masters he learned the practice of his calling—something one must understand fully, but exploit only upon one's own terms. For all that, their artistic offerings seemed to him devoid of content. The refinement of these masters gave his wild temperament little pleasure. In the words of the philosopher, he felt one must mix a little folly into all this wisdom. He saw only manual dexterity and superficial sensuality. His sense of beauty found in this art only a representation of the sensual wish, something mundane and bourgeois which was repugnant to his soul. What he missed was the spiritual.

The need to believe with all his sense-delighted soul moved him just as strongly as did the compulsion to give this need outward expression. For a long time his never-satisfied spirit had been repelled by these exaggerations, excessively good or excessively bad as the case might be, of the various schools. Their constant concern with morality struck him as a downright outrage. He had certain wishes and experienced many inquietudes; he discovered certain interlinkages that horrified him. Religion did not explain them for him, science was silent. Now his unsatiated soul, thirsting for knowledge, drew him to the deepest abysses of these superstitious ideas, and he found them rich and comforting. The basic element of his artistic creativity showed itself; sculptures that were condemned came into being, grand of scale, passionate, clumsy, and yet perfect. Superstition held mastery here.

The Atouas of the Nonka Island girl, the Zemeens of the Caribs, the refined and yet repellent idols of the African Negroes, the tree and house fetishes—in fact all the multitude of gods that symbolically reproduced the phenomena of Nature, had drawn his longing and perceptive imaginative powers. He lives by their stone altars, by the statues of their gods and by the pictures of fetishes dedicated to them as offerings: gods of war and of fertility with gigantic sexual organs, a tender female face brought to the god of love by an unfortunate lover, an antique dancer with deep-set eyes in lascivious attitude with pointed pendulous breasts, and other divinities innumerable.

When we see these ancient portrayals, which are younger than ourselves, Archipenko is illuminated.

Following only the artistic conception of their creators, he has understood by inspiration what the artist can learn from this art.

He was not satisfied to see in sculpture a mere art of imitation or of suggestion. He has created votive images as an expression of his inmost thought which he has brought as an offering to his wishes, while listening only to his modest, wonderfully child-like soul. He has worked no longer for the exclusive entertainment of the eye, but for his superstitious spirit adroit in formal abstractions.

He has put together fetishes which have protected him in moments of pain, and others which have called remembrances to life. He has composed remembrances of one vision or another, one gesture or another. He has let his fancy, enriched by oriental imagery, create freely, while at the same time always remaining mindful of the instruction of his European masters, who have restrained him from falling into high-handedness and have bound him to them through well-assimilated knowledge and through dexterity never carried to excess.

The art of the young Russian Archipenko who works in Paris, presses toward a new thing as yet unseen.

I was a witness to his artistic beginnings. Even in his early works one found this sudden but very gentle change, which one might call a "shifting of gears."

Archipenko builds reality, and his art approaches pure sculpture more and more.

Archipenko has the requisite talents for plastic synthesis.

The only artists in this sense are our new painters. The way lies open for an inward plastic art where all elements of beauty will be united, so far as the senses—here the eye—can grasp them. Archipenko's bold constructions mildly but expressively declare the mighty riches of this art.

Many-hued auras diffuse over and penetrate these humanized forms. The vaultings, the complementary forms, the differences in directions of the surfaces, the unlimited pedestals and heights—this is something which living structure and sculptural truth provide.

. . . .

Aside from a couple of very agitated and confusing figures, sculpture has hitherto been only a *melody*. The works of Archipenko are *harmony*—its first chords.

(*Der Sturm.* Siebzehnte Ausstellung:
Alexander Archipenko.
Exhibition catalogue, March 1914.
Translated by H. Bartlett Wells)

Alexander Archipenko

by Guy Habasque (1961)

Alexander Archipenko is perhaps the most forgotten and assuredly one of the most disregarded among the innovators of the beginning of the twentieth century. Yet as creator of forms and of techniques which were resolutely new, he was justly considered the principal front-rank man of avant-garde sculpture in the years before the first World War, and his contributions to the salons loosed much more passion than did those of Brancusi or Duchamp-Villon; for, more than any other, he personified at that time revolutionary audacity and rupture with traditional values.

Born at Kiev in 1887, Archipenko had studied painting and sculpture at the school of fine arts there, then at Moscow where he worked for about two years. Aware, like the majority of young Russian artists, of the reputation Paris then enjoyed for intellectual effervescence and complete esthetic freedom, he soon decided to come and pursue his studies there, and enrolled at the Ecole des Beaux-Arts where, however, he remained only a short time, preferring to perfect his artistic instruction in the museums, especially the Louvre which he visited frequently, and to work according to his own tastes.

The atmosphere he found at Paris was propitious for the most venturesome research. Sculpture was still lagging seriously as compared with painting. Rodin, growing old and covered with glory, was exercising a paralyzing influence upon the young, for whom only two courses seemed to be open, that laid down by the Master or by Medardo Rosso and the always flourishing neoclassical trend. Indeed, the only really new and valuable researches at that time were those—very few in number, to be sure, and practically unknown— by painters such as Matisse and above all Picasso and Derain. But Archipenko did not know any of them. Living at la Ruche, that city of artists in the Passage de Danzig which is famous today, he was rather closely linked with Fernand Léger and he also frequented the little group of Russian artists who lived there, as well as those of the Russian Academy in the Avenue du Maine. Yet it does not seem that any of the latter had the least share in his orientation. He set to work without a master and without a counselor.

Starting with his first Paris works, Archipenko demonstrated a clearly defined will to break from both neo-classicism and impressionism. There is no trace of the academic, nor any trace of an attempt to animate forms through subtlety of modeling, no "trick of dexterity" in detail in the sculptures of 1909 and 1910, which all still have the nude as their subject. To be truthful about it, one would seek in vain to discover any influence, or even equivalence, among them. The style is already absolutely personal, as remote from that of Duchamp-Villon as from that of Brancusi at the time. In it a violently expressive figuration is combined with a very marked stylization of forms, the first dominating in certain works and the second in others, without its yet being possible to discern which will end by taking the upper hand. In the *Baby,* the *Woman and Child,* or the *Torso* of 1909, for example, the accent is placed upon the expressive value of the forms and the attitudes. Volumes are simplified, but the figurative element is preponderant. It is the same in 1910 in the *Salome* or the *Kiss* which, compared with the work of Brancusi, become a little literary, so much does dramatic intensity seem to have been sought in them. Although they recall today certain sculptures of much later date, ones of Adam for example (in particular, the *Great Reclining Figure* of 1943), the works of this type appear in the light of hindsight as being a great deal less new and fecund than those in which the figuration is deliberately sacrificed to plastic research. In these latter, indeed, volumes are reduced to essentials, and forms are schematized with a vigor unprecedented in occidental sculpture. One almost has difficulty in believing that works like the *Poet* of the Fritz Bienert collection in Dresden; the *Suzanne* of the Museum of Pasadena, which forecasts the most audacious of Laurens; *Seated Figure* of the Museum of Modern Art in Stockholm; or, above all, the *Black Seated Torso* [Plate 9] date from 1909, so modern are they already in look and in spirit. One does not seek to depreciate the talent and the merit of such a great artist as Raymond Duchamp-Villon when one points out in passing that these last two sculptures precede by almost five years his *Seated Woman*, with which they share the same qualities of formal purity and equilibrium. The *Study for a Ceiling*, a bas-relief executed in 1910, for its part anticipates (with less power, it is true) the 1913 bas-reliefs of the same Duchamp-Villon himself such as the *Cat* or the *Lovers*. It was finally the tendency toward stripping down that was to triumph over the expressionism of the first stages, and toward the end of 1910 Archipenko, freed from every realistic or sentimental concern, dedicated himself to the solution of still-untouched plastic problems.

Of these, the first was that of full volume, a problem the importance of which is universally recognized today. One of the first to do so, along with Brancusi, Archipenko was concerned for the intrinsic value of mass, aside from any representative aim. Even though, like Brancusi, he had always retained a figurative point of departure, works like the *Hero* of the Darmstadt Museum (1910), the *Seated Woman* of the Tel Aviv Museum (1911), or the *Bather* of the former Herwarth Walden collection (1912) show that mass was defined first of all by its spatial qualities. They illustrated in advance that proposition of Laurens in which "sculpture is above all a taking possession of space, of a space limited by forms." The first experiments were surely not without influence upon Archipenko's development. They do not seem to have had such influence, on the other hand, upon Brancusi, though he did not directly face this problem until shortly thereafter, with the *Prometheus* of 1911. (The *Sleeping Muse* of 1909–1910 was merely a first approach.)

The linkage of volumes to one another concerns him equally, and he finds solutions for it which are frequently very original for the time. Thus, starting in 1910 with the first two versions of the *Silhouette* [Plate 25], he undertakes the study of flexion and rolling movement in small or intersecting volumes. These statuettes, drawn out in height, in fact present beveled forms, with sharp ridges, about which the volume of the arm rolls out in a spiral, a volume so slight and so long that it seems reduced to the thickness of a ribbon. So far as the love of height is concerned, one finds it right through the production of Archipenko, who always liked to toss out long curved lines which, after having separated or run in contrary directions, strive to rejoin at a peak. If the lines of the various *Silhouettes* of 1910 to 1913 or of the *Flat Torso* of 1914 (Museums of Tel Aviv and Philadelphia) do not achieve the purity of those of the *Maiastra* or of the *Bird in Space* of Brancusi, they nevertheless bear witness to a will to strip things to essentials which was still far from common at the beginning of the century.

But Archipenko understands how not to limit himself to one field of research or another. He glimpses many other new ways of developing mass in space. For example, he imposes upon certain of his works unusual and apparently unstable equilibriums. As early as 1909 the *Poet* flexed his body and his arms knotted above his head in a curiously oblique movement. In 1911 a statuette of chrome-plated bronze entitled *Penchée* [Plate 26] bends the schematized silhouette of a person so far as to make it take on the form of an actual quadrant of a circle. When one considers the date, one does not know what to admire more here, the audacious balance or the revolutionary stripping of the practically "abstract" volumes (in the present sense of the term). In the *Black Dancer*, also of 1911, the torso this time rests precariously upon a single leg, a little in the manner of a Praxiteles, but of a Praxiteles from which one has arbitrarily cut a leg, the volume of body being slightly shifted over the gap thus created.

One can ally with these "static" (in the etymological sense of the term) studies a whole series of other sculptures (the *Kiss* of 1911, *Two Bodies*, the *Composition with Two Persons*, the *Dance* [Plate 22] of 1912, the *Red Dance* of 1913, etc.) in which the bodies with long extended limbs bend and knot in arabesques, sometimes rather unstable, recalling a little those of the *Dance* of Matisse. But these works raise another problem which is also to be of great importance in all contemporary sculpture, that of the relationship between empty spaces and solid areas. This problem is, to be sure, not specific to the twentieth century, but since each period offers its own solution, it will not be exaggerating to say that once more Archipenko is the first to solve it in really modern fashion. In fact, the portions of space outlined by the play of the arabesques take on a new value here, and their role becomes as important as that of the solid volumes. In the *Dance* in particular, the bodies form a sort of solid framework enclosing an impalpable but perfectly visible volume.

With the first version of the *Walking Woman* in 1912 (Denver Art Museum) Archipenko is to accentuate still further this positive character of space in creating true "counter-volumes." Certain volumes, in fact—the left leg, the head, the torso—are limited *exteriorly* by the material. It is difficult to appreciate today the novelty of this solution, so much have we become used to it, but when one reflects one understands better the fact that the central empty space of this sculpture, for example, was inconceivable no more than a hundred years ago. For a man of the nineteenth century a bit of empty space had no reality; for a man of the twentieth century, on the other hand, space is a concrete living thing, endowed with positive qualities just as matter itself. And it is perhaps here that we have one of the most fundamental characteristics of contemporary sculpture. Was it not by taking cognizance of the active value of space, indeed, that Pevsner and Gabo some years later steered a totally new course? If the solution proposed by Archipenko is far from being as radical as theirs, if he has lacked above all that which will give to their solution its absolute revolutionary character—namely the affirmation of the dynamic qualities of space—it is nevertheless true that in the *Walking Woman* [*Walking,* Plate 42] we have the rough outline of a system of plastic expression entirely different from that which was in use for centuries. The mere fact that the essential part of the head is not made up of the two strips of matter which circumscribe it, but by the internal space thus created, is the material statement of an undeniable rupture with the classic spirit. This way of "signifying" the head, in fact, becomes common practice in the work of Archipenko from this year on and comes to have great influence on other sculptors, notably Henry Moore.

The study of hollow volumes moves him, moreover, to adopt in 1913 *(Woman Combing Her Hair)* [*Green Concave,* Plate 73] another technical device which we shall likewise find throughout the course of his production, that of "concave" forms. The artist has said that this mode of expression offers a meaning which is at once psychological and optical. If the theory of complementarity by means of which he justifies the materiality of *"non-being form"* is not necessarily convincing from the philosophical standpoint, this materiality has become evident in practice from the plastic standpoint. Any concave inflection of the form (provided, naturally, that it does not involve a simple hollow between two volumes) in fact immediately suggests to us the non-visible convex volume that corresponds to it.

The years 1913 and 1914 were for Archipenko perhaps the most fecund of his whole career. On the one hand he draws from his preceding experiments some of his most beautiful and most consummate works such as the *Gondolier* [Plate 47] and above all *Boxers* [Plate 50], which ranks among the most representative works of modern sculpture. On the other hand, he opens up two new research fields in which he rapidly achieves results the influence of which is to be considerable: polychromy and constructions.

If polychromy is not a novelty, one must recognize that it had almost completely disappeared from Western sculpture after the seventeenth century and that the spirit in which it is resumed proves to be rather different from that of the various past attempts. Form and color, Archipenko asserts, are so closely linked that they form an indissoluble whole and should be considered as two aspects of a single reality, just as are matter and energy in modern physics. One of the very first essays along this line, the *Carrousel Pierrot* of 1913, is even today the most convincing example of his entire production. The contrasts of the vivid lacquered colors exercise in it an undeniable influence upon the forms and guarantee the work a particularly effective dynamism.

The constructions for their part represent one of the most original contributions of Archipenko to the history of sculpture. Starting with the first one, in 1912—the first version of *Medrano*—Archipenko demonstrates a well-settled will to remake totally the traditional material of sculpture.

Here lacquered wood sustains a much more vivid and suggestive polychromy while the easier working of the material makes it possible to refine the linking of volumes and in case of need, as Léger would have said, to "de-wood" them. Even if carried out in a number of pieces, a sculpture in stone, bronze, or plaster always gives the impression of forming a single mass. The assembling of elements which are related and which are sharply differentiated, on the contrary, guarantees the constructions a greater independence among the various volumes and considerably lightens the whole. Plywood and metal make it possible to cut certain volumes or to introduce, as in *Medrano II* and *Woman at Her Toilet* (1914) [*Woman Before a Mirror,* Plate 37], plane surfaces of very slight thickness, giving birth to a space sharply different from that determined by traditional masses. Metal and glass furthermore create effects of transparency or reflection which had thitherto been impossible to obtain. The immateriality of certain planes is further reinforced in *Medrano II* by the lace of the skirt and above all in *Medrano I* (which is actually a great deal more audacious than the second version) by the introduction of a semicircle of iron wire which circumscribes and suggests, without representing, the outline of the right shoulder.

But it is probably the *Head* (1914) [Plate 39], a work unfortunately destroyed during the war of 1914–1918, that was the most modern in spirit and the most interesting of all his constructions. This is owing not merely to the excellent way in which the figurative content "informed" the plastic image, but also because the technique used resolved problems with revolutionary and still important novelty. The head, composed of three cones of sheet iron and some superimposed planes of wood and glass, was set in the center of a circular base in front of a semi-cylinder (constituting a background) which, being perfectly polished, reflected spots of colors painted upon the back side of the plane surfaces of the head. Luminous reflection, the immateriality and mobility of color, even today (as we know) preoccupy some of the most advanced artists.

Let us not go overboard here. We do not propose to exaggerate the importance of Archipenko. Others who came after him or limited themselves to restricted fields have played a part which was often more considerable. It is nonetheless true that from the historical standpoint he was the first to touch upon the majority of the problems raised by contemporary sculptors and that he almost always found for them solutions which had previously been unknown. This is justice which is too rarely done him. If one sets up a short comparative panorama of sculpture on the eve of the first World War, one sees that the only other artists who had then already produced works which one can still today classify as modern were Brancusi, Duchamp-Villon, and Boccioni. But at that Brancusi had no more than a few achievements behind him, admirable though they were (the *Kiss, Prometheus,* the *Maiastra, Mlle Pogany,* the *Penguins*), and the most advanced sculptures of Duchamp-Villon (*Maggy,* the *Seated Woman,* and above all the great *Horse* of 1914) did not go beyond those of Archipenko of 1912 in novelty. Only Boccioni had been able to create an original and—whatever one may think of his deeper value—modern style. At that time Lipchitz, Zadkine, Laurens, Czaky, Chauvin, or Gargallo had to their credit no more than starts, frequently promising enough, but still too fragmentary for one to compare their achievements with those of the other men. Lehmbruck and Epstein were working in very different directions and ones far more respectful of established conventions. As for the American Elie Nadelman, then fairly well known, his modernism consisted in representing persons clothed and coiffed as in everyday life.

In fact, one must wait for the first works of Pevsner and Gabo, the bursting into bloom of the talent of Laurens and the other cubists, and the first steps of artists such as Arp, Gonzalez, or Vantongerloo, before one is able really to discern other original trends. From that time Archipenko was rapidly to lose the preponderant position he had previously occupied among the avant-garde.

One notices, moreover, a sharp shift in his esthetic outlook about that time. He exploits more completely his pre-war discoveries and henceforward tries above all to create a style for himself. He pursued the problem of concave planes to notable depths, then that of hollow volumes and the equilibrium of empty spaces and solid matter which, as with reflections and polychromy, constituted so many techniques which one finds henceforward through the whole course of his production, now separately, now conjointly. Indeed, from 1915 on one can discern in his works the first manifestations of a will toward synthesis. In the sculpto-paintings of 1915–1920, for example, he uses at the same time the acquired assets of his polychrome sculptures and his constructions, to which he adds about 1918 some elements drawn from his concave sculptures and hollow volumes. But Archipenko was twice to go beyond the limits set by his earlier researches: first in 1924, with the invention of *Archipentura* [Plate 107], again in 1947 with the achievement of transparent luminous sculptures.

"Archipentura," he himself said, "is a machine conceived in order to produce the illusion of movement by a painted subject"; it is "a new art form which makes use of time and space. So Archipentura paints time." (*Archipenko: Fifty Creative Years*, pp. 65–67.) This extraordinary engine produces a movement which is still rather rudimentary, but its importance is considerable if one cares to take into account the date of its birth. Along with the Optical Machines of Marcel Duchamp, it in fact constitutes one of the very first attempts to introduce "real" movement into a work of art. Archipenko unfortunately did not follow up this experiment. The luminous sculptures are of a simpler though very interesting conception. These are sculptures analogous to the others, based on the same themes (concave surfaces, empty spaces, etc.) but carved in thick sheets of plexiglass, a material which ensures perfect transparency of the mass without producing the same refraction phenomena as glass, and moreover offering excellent light conductivity. Thanks to the use of a source of light hidden in a base, the sculpture seems to have become petrified in a material which is itself luminous.

In spite of these two important exceptions, the fact remains that Archipenko's great creative period came before the First World War. Not that everything had been said then, but he had already delivered the essence of his message and proposed solutions which his later works could do little more than refine or perfect. Besides, an artist's vein of creativity is not inexhaustible and the five years from 1909 through 1914 are so full of all kinds of discoveries that they suffice to assure him a prominent place in the birth of modern sculpture. True, it is possible to have reservations about the level of the quality of some of his works, especially recent ones; one may regret that the figurative element now and then obstructs the full development of the sculptural expression, but one cannot deny that Archipenko was one of the principal innovators of the beginning of the century.*

At the time the public and critics did not let themselves be deluded. They understood at once that the revolutionary character of his works was inevitably to strike traditional sculpture a mortal blow. Those who have the curiosity to leaf through the press of those decisive years will be able to assert that aside from Picasso no artist was so violently attacked, so systematically denigrated and mocked, as was Archipenko. But some better-informed critics faithfully sustained his efforts, starting with the *Salon des Independants* of 1911 where his *New Eve* had drawn their attention. André Salmon and Guillaume Apollinaire in particular lost no occasion to break a lance in his favor.

In 1914 Archipenko exhibited at the *Independants* some of his newest and most important works: the *Carrousel Pierrot*, the *Gondolier* [Plate 47], the *Boxers* [Plate 50], and *Medrano II*. There was a general hue and cry. "This is how I should like to describe the *Gondolier* of M. Archipenko," wrote, for example, Edouard Helsey in the Journal (2 March 1914, page 1, C)—"a bronze figure which recalls at one and the same time a broom, a bottle nipple, a propeller blade, a broken street-lamp, a dead tree branch. Alas! how is one to

---

* *Editor's note:* When Habasque wrote this essay in 1960, he had not viewed many of Archipenko's then recent sculpture. In addition, Archipenko created eleven sculptures from 1960 until his death in 1964, many of which are major works in the artist's *œuvre*. As art historian Frederick Wight has stated, "... his [Archipenko's] two periods of greatest inventiveness are the first and last decades of his life as an artist."

render in words this sage incoherence! Only photography could give a remote idea of these original achievements."

But even before the vernissage Apollinaire had been asserting the contrary: "The most novel and attractive offering is in my opinion that of Archipenko—polychrome sculptures executed in various materials: glass, wood, iron combined in the newest and most felicitous way." (*L'Intransigeant*, 28 February 1914, page 1, F.) It would appear that this eulogy exasperated his journalistic colleagues and the next day one of them, named Emile Delfin, published a pretty sharp review of the vernissage which ended with these sentences: "This year I shall recommend to you only a charming innovation destined, I believe, to be most enviably successful. I mean statues in gondolized (and gondolizing) sheet iron, varnished, tinted, an accumulation of tubing and smokestacks, whirls with wafers, turning plates, gutters, and latrine boxes, all set up in unstable equilibrium on a base bearing the signature of the perpetrator and the title of the work exhibited." (Idem, 1 March, page 1, DE.) Was his article already in or did Apollinaire voluntarily let it pass through? In any case, here is what he wrote without circumlocution:

Rooms XI and IX: Here is where you will see the sculptures of Archipenko; one of them is made of various materials, glass, zinc, wood, all polychromed. This is a very great effort to escape from the conventional in sculpture. With excuses to those of my colleagues who are so sure they know esthetic truth that they do not even mention such a surprising thing, executed in so fluent and graceful a manner, I am happy to report all the pleasure the sight of so delicate a work occasioned me. The second polychrome statue exhibited in the center of Room IX is no less interesting, and I am very sorry for those who fail to be affected by the charm and elegance of this gondolier, a black and slender statue which is exhibited in Room XI. (Idem, 2 March, page 2, A.)

But before seeing these lines on the second page readers might contemplate on the first a fine photograph of *Medrano* with this simple commentary: "We reproduce a photograph of the work of art (?) which our collaborator Guillaume Apollinaire evaluates further on, upon his own responsibility." What was involved here was in other words a public disavowal on the part of his own paper. In any case, that is how Apollinaire interpreted it. Summoned in to give account of himself by Leon Bailby, the publisher of *L'Intransigeant,* he lost his patience and handed in his resignation.

This recalling of polemics now outworn does not merely fix a point in history. It also brings into full light the double part of revolutionary and of guide which Archipenko then played—a part the importance of which should not be underestimated by anyone who wants to get a clear and objective idea of the birth and the evolution of contemporary sculpture. From this point of view, it indeed seems that it is time to reconsider the rather minor position which is generally accorded to this artist.

(This essay was first published in *L'Œil*, in June 1961, and is reproduced in this catalogue with the permission of the editors of *L'Œil*. Translated by H. Bartlett Wells)

The Concave and Void

by Alexander Archipenko

In order to explain the spiritual value of my concave, we must consider the psychological side of this new sculptural element. It is evident that in sculpture each point of the surface should have meaning and be related to millions of other points of the surface. Likewise, relief and concave are reciprocally integrated. It is exactly as in music; each note has its psychological significance while it is related to every other note and pause in the composition. So in my sculpture, all concaves have optical and psychological significance, while related to other relief parts. In describing optical effects, I should mention the following episode.

In 1927 I exhibited in the Denver Museum. A conservative Trustee, guided around the exhibition by Mr. Rönebek, who was then Director, objected to the idea of concave sculpture. He pointed to my statue which was concave and said: "I prefer this statue with normal form, no concave riddles!" Mr. Rönebek replied: "But this statue *is* concave!" The optical illusion is a consequence of the frontal light under which the concave and convex will have similar effects. The deepest and highest forms will have similar highlights in the center. Both forms will produce similar effects, especially on shiny surfaces.

The psychological significance of concaves in my sculpture derives from creative sources and provokes creative action. They are perceptible as symbols of the absent form and are subject to association and relativity. We cannot deny that in our psychological make-up the positive and the negative are of identical force and we merely apply them in different proportions according to our orientation and interest in a particular case. In our daily lives our "yes" and "no" are both centered around the same point of interest and used as positive or negative decisions according to our personal advantage. All positive and negative by the nature of polarity eventually become one. There is no concave form without a convex; there is no convex without a concave. Both elements are fused into one significant ensemble. In the creative process, as in life itself, the reality of the negative is a conceptual imprint of the absent positive.

It is not exactly the presence of a thing but rather the absence of it that becomes the cause and impulse for creative motivation. This process exists in nature as latent force and is the fundamental creative inducer of new organic life. Nature creates that which is not yet there. The apprehension and use of this principle by an individual may guide him to the understanding of many transcendental values of art and life.

It should be pointed out that the materiality of the non-existent is indeed the most vital concept; but it is also a dangerously subtle creative element of art. Without a clear comprehension of it and without correct technical execution, it is easy to fall into absurdity. For instance, drilling meaningless holes into a statue or digging senseless cavities if they are not symbolical or associative, cannot serve as substitutes and become absurd. The piercing of a hole in a kidney-like shape is very far from the spiritual meaning of the symbolization of absent reality. The amorphous part of the canvas or the amorphous unspeaking masses are symbols of creative impotence rather than of creative power. Indeed, a mannerism or a toying with empty accidental happenings, or buffoonery, will never lift a work of art toward a spiritual quality.

Sculpto-Painting

by Alexander Archipenko

Sculpto-painting is not only a renaissance of the vanished tendency to unite form and color; it is rather a new medium of art, due to a specific conjunction and amalgamation of materials, forms and colors. Esthetically and technically, sculpto-paintings are entirely different from the colored reliefs à la Della Robbia or the Egyptian and Assyrian. The novelty does not lie in the fact that sculpto-paintings are reliefs, but in the fact that stylistically, conceptionally and esthetically they are new, as a result of entirely new materials and techniques.

Sculpto-painting is more effective and diverse in character than the usual painting or uncolored sculpture. The unification of color and form does not interfere with spiritualization; on the contrary, it facilitates the expression of the abstract in this medium. There is here no naturalistic coloration such as mannequins with blue eyes, black eyebrows or red lips. It is an entirely different technico-esthetic problem which sculpto-painting resolves while engaged in dealing with the abstract, spiritual or symbolic.

In sculpto-painting, as in usual painting, a pattern of color can be limited by sharp contours, or it can be blended with the neighboring colors to become a contourless area. The advantage of sculpto-painting over the usual painting is that on the painted flat area sculptured reliefs or concave forms are added as integral parts of the compositional effect and meaning.

(This extract and the preceding one are from
Archipenko: Fifty Creative Years 1908–1958)

Polychrome Manifesto

by Alexander Archipenko

What is the cause of the weakening of the spirit which in the past guided artists in the creation of magnificent polychrome sculpture?

Contemporary sculptors, of course, are not color-blind. However, there are no polychrome sculptures on display. Contemporary artists and those connected with art seem to be unaware of and to omit the spiritual and esthetic value intrinsic in the unity of colors with forms. There is no evidence of conscious penetration beyond impoverished sculpture, disrobed of colors. What is the cause of the deterioration of polychrome sculpture? Is it the consequence of the irrational theory which teaches that pure form is in mono-colored matter only? Do we not admire the multicolored forms in birds and flowers, etc.? When one looks in the mirror does one not see himself as form and colors?

In polychromy there is limitless possibility for inventions corresponding to modern creative conceptions and spirit. The tradition of colored wax mannikins is fortunately over, and it is useless to revive the stylistic character of Egyptian polychromy, or Tanagra, or that of the extraordinary Northwest American Indian, or Australian Bushman. It is senseless to follow them because the modern era is not inspired by their mythology, but uses totally new life conceptions and methods for creative demonstrations.

Outmoded, literary, mythological symbolism is no longer usable, but a new symbology which abstracts and spiritualizes the object must take its place, so that color-form will become synonymous with the object. Such new symbolism is essential to modern polychrome sculpture and is the consequence of modern, creative, scientific and psychological facts. Due to the progress of our civilization and new psychological scope it is natural to disregard antiquated esthetics and ideology. Polychromy should be renewed.

In our daily mobile environment colors change into forms and forms into colors and there are no forms without colors; also, there are more multicolored forms than mono-colored. Such characteristics of our environment should finally provoke endless creative assumptions, experiences and expressions by alerted artists.

In this modern era matter alone is acknowledged not to be a totality; natural creative energy with its complex transformations is considered to be the prime cause of evolution. It is, therefore, evident that the reciprocal infusions of colors-forms in polychromy are comparable to the concept of transformative energy. Such energy constitutes the life of polychrome art. It is this art of interfusing which is the lost secret, hidden in ancient polychromy which is far richer than the contemporary non-colored sculpture.

Spiritually, esthetically, emotionally, creatively and symbolically, the form-color interactions are as rich as the variations in a symphony, in which one musical phrase interfuses with another, thereby evoking multiple reactions in the individual.

New polychromy consists of a new esthetic and technique which unifies forms with colors. Their reciprocal overlapping and interfusion, the domination of one over another, their harmony or contrast and their rhythm are all adjustable according to the symbolic or stylistic problems.

Polychromy is fully adaptable for three-dimensional sculpture, reliefs, construction in diverse materials, for sculpto-painting, for disciplined abstractions, for the expression of relativity and for symbolical interpretations which are indirect representations of the object.

Polychrome sculpture, like nature, produces an infinite variety of effects and has more potential and vitality than flat painting or mono-colored sculpture, since the reality of forms produces natural light and shadow in which the patterns of colors automatically change their nuances.

This is a new way of transmitting creative messages. This is a new optical language.

Creative awareness of color-form will lead a receptive individual to establish many subtleties and spiritual reactions through polychrome sculpture. The same awareness may help sensitive individuals to grasp these creative messages.

The modern polychrome method reflects contemporary conceptions of creative transformations of material things and gives them a spiritual aspect. A creative artist must rely on his competence and orientations in this matter, since the new principles of polychrome art are still not yet propagated. Also, the knowledge and ability for analysis and judgment of this new art is still not developed in the contemporary literature on art.

(From *Archipenko:
Fifty Creative Years 1908–1958*)

*Archipenko Memorial
Retrospective at the National
Collection of Fine Arts,
Smithsonian Institution, summer, 1968*

25

1

2

3

4

5

1. *Archipenko's mother,*
Poroskovia Wassilievna
Machova Archipenko, Kiev
2. *Archipenko's father, Porfiry*
Antonovich Archipenko, Kiev
3. *Alexander (left) and brother,*
Eugene, Kiev, 1890
4. *Alexander, Kiev, 1894*
5. *Alexander, Kiev, circa 1900*
6. *Eugene, Kiev, 1902*
7. *Prayer, 1907, tempera, hand*
carved and gilded, 8 × 8¼"
8. *Adam and Eve, 1908, bronze,*
19¾" (cat. 1) (Parenthetical
number refers to list of works
starting page 114)

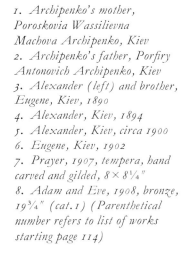

6

7

9

10

11

ARCHIPENKO
L'AMOUR DES BÊTES
OU LA FEMME QUI NE FAIT QU'UN
AVEC SON CHAT

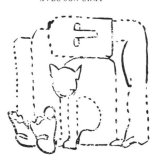

13   CHERCHEZ LA FEMME!
PAR ARCHIPENKO

12

9. *Sculpting Black Seated Torso,
1909 (cat.4)*
10. *Postcard from Le Fauconnier
addressed to Archipenko at
36, rue des Artistes, Paris, 1913*
11. *In Moscow, 1907, just prior
to leaving for Paris*
12. *With friends in Paris, 1909*
13. *1911 Parisian newspaper
caricature of Woman with Cat
for Salon d'Automne review*
14. *Woman with Cat, 1910,
bronze, 13¼" (cat.6)*

14

Призыв. сп. 190_ г. № 990 с/_ уч.

СВИДѢТЕЛЬСТВО

О ЯВКѢ КЪ ИСПОЛНЕНІЮ ВОИНСКОЙ ПОВИННОСТИ.

(БЕЗСРОЧНОЕ)

Васильковскій мѣщанинъ Архипенко Александръ Парфентіевъ явился къ исполненію воинской повинности при призывѣ 190_ г. и по вынотому имъ № _четыреста двадцать второму_ жеребья, подлежалъ поступленію на службу въ войска, но, по освидѣтельствованію, признанъ совершенно неспособнымъ къ военной службѣ, а потому освобожденъ навсегда отъ службы

Выдано Васильковскимъ уѣзднымъ по воинской повинности Присутствіемъ _Ноября 20_ дня 190_ г. за № ___

Предсѣдатель Присутствія _[подпись]_

Дѣлопроизводитель _[подпись]_

[штамп]

20 сентября 1918 г. за № 69894 на
что актъ выдана паспорт
ная книжка

[подпись]

Васильковъ, Тип. Дубовика.

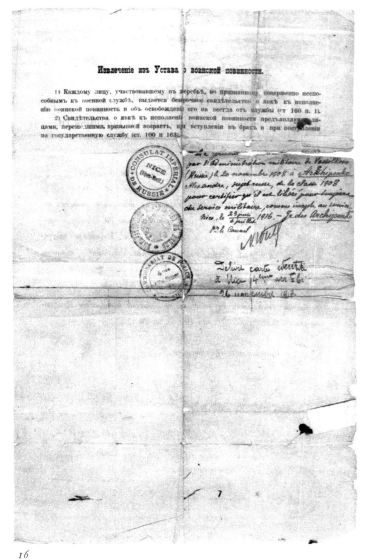

15

16

15. Certificate, Moscow, 1908, exempting Archipenko from military service, permitting departure from Russia
16. Reverse
17. Alien residence certificate, Paris, 1909
18. Alien residence certificate, for move to Nice from Paris, 9 February 1914

(Mod. 181.)

RÉPUBLIQUE FRANÇAISE

PRÉFECTURE DE POLICE

№ 157270

VILLE DE PARIS

1re DIVISION

4e BUREAU

En exécution du décret du 2 octobre 1888, Par devant nous, Préfet de Police, s'est présenté le sieur Archipenko Alexandre

Fils de Sarphir et de Prascovia Machowa

Né le 30 Mai 1887 à Kiew Russie

Nationalité : Russe

Dernier domicile : Berlin

Profession : Etudiant

Marié à

Enfants mineurs :

Pièces justificatives : Passeport

Lequel nous a déclaré fixer sa résidence à Paris rue St Louis en l'Ile, nº 62

département de la Seine.

Signature du déclarant,

Fait à Paris, le 13 Juillet 1909

Pour le Préfet de Police,

NOTA. — Chaque fois que les Étrangers changent de domicile ou quittent le Département de la Seine, ils doivent en informer la Préfecture de Police.

17

№ 7294

RÉPUBLIQUE FRANÇAISE

DÉPARTEMENT des Alpes-Maritimes — COMMUNE DE NICE — ARRONDISSEMENT DE NICE

EXTRAIT DU REGISTRE D'IMMATRICULATION

Application de la Loi du 8 Août 1893

En exécution de la loi du 8 Août 1893, par devant nous, Maire de la commune de Nice, s'est présenté le sieur :

Nom et Prénoms : Archipenko Alexandre

Lieu de naissance : Kiew (Russie)

Date de la naissance : 30 mai 1887

Nationalité : Russe

Fils de Sarphir

Et de Machowa Prascovia

Marié ou veuf :

Marié à (1) Célibataire

Enfant (2) 1.
2.
3.
4.
5.
6.

lequel nous a déclaré être arrivé le 9 février 1914 de Paris dans cette commune pour y exercer (3) artiste peintre Rue Cronstadt, 13

Il a justifié de son identité conformément aux dispositions de l'article 1er de la loi, en produisant à l'appui de sa déclaration (4) 1° Déclaration antérieure de Paris du Décret du 2 8bre 1888 [illegible] à l'École des Beaux Arts ; 2° certificat militaire d'exemption

Fait à Nice, le 7 juillet 191[illegible]

Pour le Maire,
Le Commissaire Central, délégué

(1) Nom, prénoms, âge et nationalité de la femme.
(2) Nom, prénoms, sexe, âge et nationalité de chacun des enfants mineurs.
(3) Indiquer la nature de la profession, du commerce et de l'industrie que l'étranger compte exercer.
(4) Indiquer la nature des pièces justificatives, produites à l'appui de la déclaration.

NOTA. — Les visas pour cause de changements de résidence doivent être inscrits au verso du présent extrait d'immatriculation, avec application du cachet de la mairie.

18

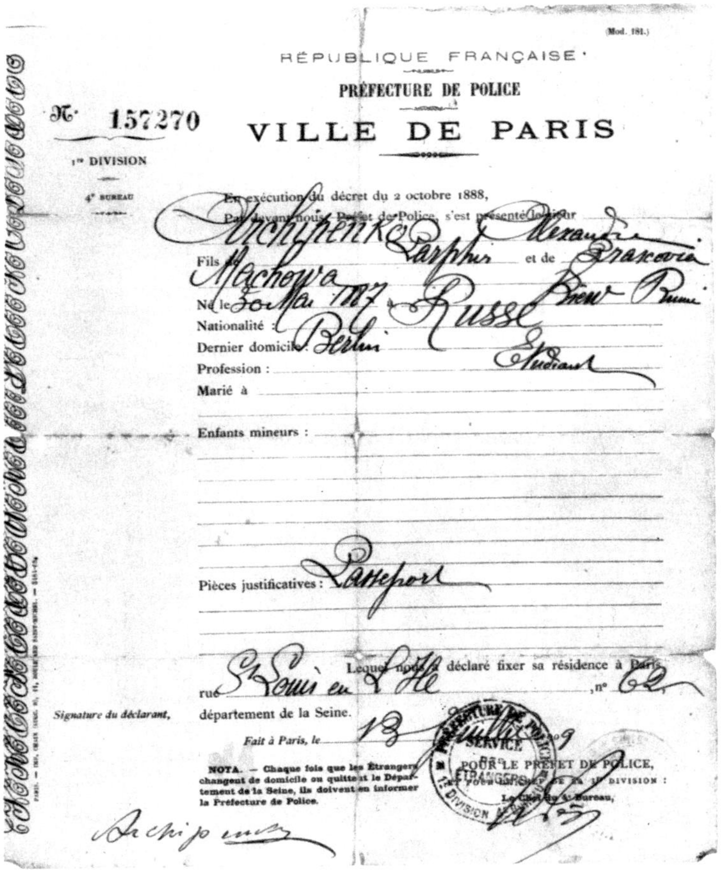

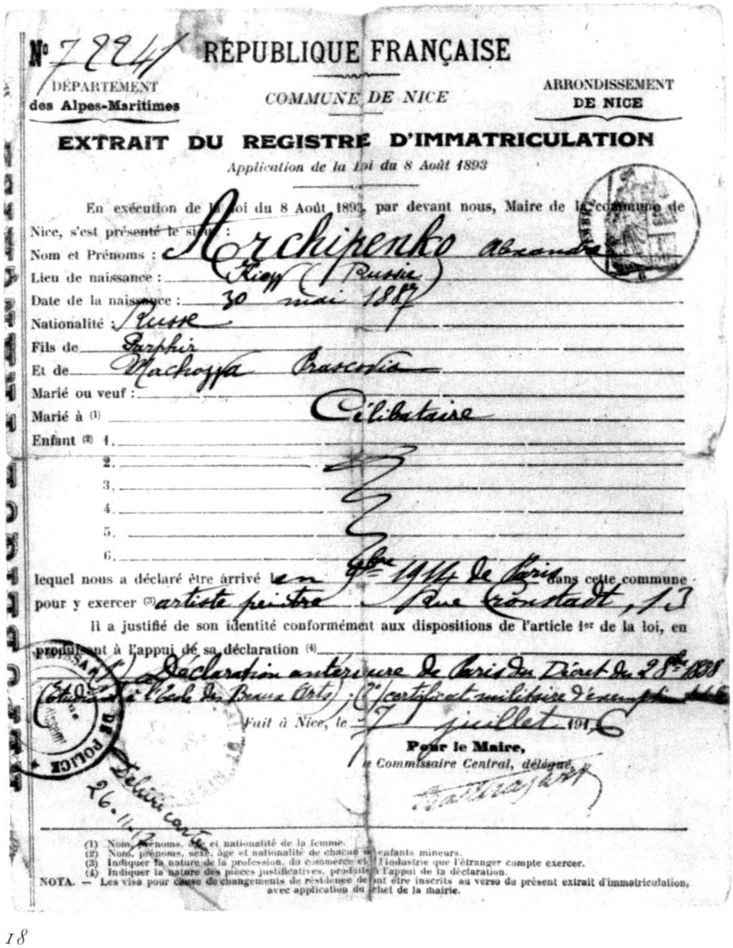

20

19

19. *Draped Woman, 1911,
bronze, 22″ (cat. 8)*
20. *Mother and Child,
1910, bronze, 13¾″
(cat. 5)*
21. *Madonna of the Rocks,
1912, bronze, 20¼″ (cat. 9)*

The Gothic elongation and distortion emanate from religious ideas, ecstasy and gravitation toward highly soaring divine power. The Egyptian, Gothic and modern styles, by their leaning toward creative abstract qualities, prove that they are subordinated to the same dynamism of nature with its perpetual transforming power which they set out to express.

Unlike past eras, our contemporary mechanization and speed for the economy of time are the causes for the rapid changes of forms in modern art. The production of the Egyptian style existed over 5,000 years; the Gothic, 500; modern Cubism, 10 years. Now in our tempo, art seems to be deteriorating into a seasonal performance. The history of art has known no such turbulent period of varied stylistic experimentation as in the present day.

As a retrograde mind cannot stop the avalanche of scientific invention, so retrograde or hostile criticism cannot affect artistic stylistic inventions. In fact, no criticism in general can make or destroy the historical value of a work of art, since the history of art is fixed by the spiritual content of the work itself, not by the magazine which prints favorable or poisonous articles.

Archipenko

3

2. Dance, 1912, bronze,
4⅛" (cat. 12)
3. Cover of English
ublication, "The Sketch,"
. October 1913, with
arning to citizenry
4. Caricature of Silhouette,
'enice, 1920
5. Silhouette, 1910,
ronze, 17"
6. Penchée, 1911, bronze,
5⁄8"

26

24   *25*

27

Sturm Bilderbücher

II
Alexander Archipenko

Verlag Der Sturm | Berlin *1913*

28

My ancestors, the same as the Russians, availed themselves in the past of Byzantine and Oriental influences. I like Byzantine and Oriental art, in fact all that is of genius in every country and of all times, and my real tradition is found everywhere—in the genius of human creation. There is no nationality in my creations. In that respect, I am no more Ukrainian than I am Chinese. I am no one person.

Archipenko

30

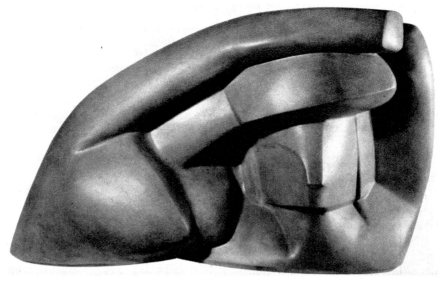

33

32

34

30. *Repose, 1911, bronze,*
13½ × 14½" (cat.7).
Exhibited in Armory Show
31. *Caricature of Family Life,*
Armory Show review,
"The World," New York,
17 February 1913
32. *View of Armory Show,*
New York, 1913
33. *Family Life, 1935, bronze*
(after design of 1912),
18 × 31" (cat.48)
34. *Six-foot terra cotta*
of Family Life, 1912, exhibited
in Armory Show.
(Destroyed WWI)
35. *Family Life, 1912,*
bronze, 22" (cat.10)

35

1

The elements of sculpto-painting are applied not only to panels, but also to constructions and to three-dimensional sculpture. In such cases the roundness of the statue becomes a formed background on which patterns of color are applied. This is a three-dimensional polychrome sculpture. Some compositions require the pattern of color to be the same as the shape of the raised or lowered forms. The art of sculpto-painting proves to be refined and complex and is not easily grasped by conservatives or laymen. This expansive form of art, under the tool of the uninitiated, may dwindle to naught, especially if only one element of sculpto-painting is used. For instance, there would be no spiritual depth if one were to cut the shape of a kidney from a board, nail it to a panel, and paint all in one color.

Archipenko

36

37

*36. In his atelier, Paris,
circa 1913 (at age 26)
37. Woman in Front of Mirror,
1914, glass, wood, metal, and
mirror, 7 feet. Torso and head are
reflected in mirror.
(Destroyed WWI)
38. Head, 1913, bronze, 14⅞"
(cat. 15). Sketch for Woman
in Front of Mirror*

39

40

41

39. *Head, 1914, 22".
Construction installed in
center of disc. Background is
niche of polished bent metal,
reflecting multiple spots of
different colors painted on back
of planes. Head is four superimposed planes of different
patterns, some in glass, some in
wood. (Destroyed WWI)*
40. *Russian caricature, 1915,
of Head as Wilhelm II*
41. *"La Tête" by Blaise
Cendrars, Nice, 1918*
42. *Walking, 1912, bronze,
52½" (cat.11)*
43. *Woman with Fan, 1914,
polychromed bronze relief,
35¾" (cat.22)*

42

43

44

45

46

46. *Walking Soldier, 1917, polychromed bronze, 46" (cat. 32)*
47. *Gondolier, 1914, bronze, 64" (cat. 20)*
48. *Caricatures of (from left to right) Gondolier, Medrano I, Carrousel Pierrot, and distorting of Apollinaire's name, Paris, 7 March 1914*
49. *Poem referring to Gondolier, Paris, 1914*

47

48

AU SALON DES INDÉPENDANTS

Chacun se souvient encore
Du brave douanier Rousseau,
De la faune et de la flore
Chefs-d'œuvre de son pinceau !

Des enfants à jambes tortes,
Sans gabarit ni cerveau,
Qui tenaient, en quelque sorte,
De la grenouille et du veau,

Des seigneurs et des concierges,
Ainsi que des amoureux,
Errant en des forêts vierges
Parmi des tigres affreux...

Croyez que l'excellent homme
N'était du tout un' farceur.
Il ne se donnait pas comme
Un Simon le Précurseur.

Il ne souillait pas sa toile,
Ainsi que Boronali
Fit plus tard, et dont l'étoile,
Hélas ! a trop tôt pâli !

Non. Sa peinture était celle
D'un enfant, au résumé,
D'une ingénuité telle,
Que l'on était désarmé.

Mais chose des plus grièves,
Nous constatons aujourd'hui
Qu'il a fait quelques élèves
Qui vont raffinant sur lui,

Et sottise non pareille !
Vous accrocheront un nez
A la place de l'oreille,
Pour n'être point surannés...

Ce qui n'était qu'impuissance
Chez le maître en question,
Chez eux n'est plus que licence
Et mystification.

Pardon !... du côté sculpture,
Dans ce même bâtiment,
Un se montre — sur facture —
Très sincère, évidemment.

C'est celui qui, cette année,
Nous fait avec des tuyaux
De poêle, de cheminée,
Entr'autres matériaux,

Une sorte de bonhomme,
Lequel n'est pas dans un sac,
Mais qui représente, en somme,
Un « gondolier », tout à trac.

Au moins ce sculpteur est drôle,
Il ne cache pas son jeu ;
Et son gondolier en tôle
A la valeur d'un aveu :

En effet, le doux artiste
A tout simplement voulu
Nous prouver qu'il est fumiste,
Mais c'était bien superflu.

Après tout, sombres esthètes,
J'ai comme un vague soupçon
Que vous vous payez nos têtes,
Et vous avez bien raison,

Puisqu'on trouve des critiques
Assez fous pour discuter
Vos horreurs systématiques,
Des gens pour les acheter.

RAOUL PONCHON.

49

If the form of any object is simplified to the last degree, it will inevitably become a strictly geometric shape: in painting, flat patterns; in sculpture, crystallization. We hold that it is not necessary to be a Cubist in order to simplify form into flat patterns, as is proved by Japanese prints. It is the same with the geometrization of form in the Mayan sculpture, in the art of the American Indians and of the Orientals. They were not Cubists. If all that is geometric is Cubism, then New York City is also Cubist.

As for my own work, the geometric character of three-dimensional sculptures (e.g., *Boxers,* 1913, *Gondolier,* 1914) is due to the extreme simplification of form and not to Cubist dogma. I did not take from Cubism, but added to it. At this time no other sculptor reduced forms to their fundamentally geometric structure. In spite of that, the above-mentioned sculptures are classified as Cubist, with rare objection against such classification. The same understanding should be applied to my constructions and sculpto-paintings which are geometric, not because Cubism is geometric, but because the material and technique used inevitably produced a strong geometric effect. Bent sheets of metal and the flatness of boards or glass are naturally geometric. Historically, the geometric tendency in art is as old as art itself, particularly in ornaments, Inca sculpture, American Indian, Oriental and some Negro art. Neither Cézanne nor the Cubists were the inventors of the geometric type of art; the Cubists merely centralized the concept and brought it to its purest and strongest expression by the extreme simplification of patterns.

Archipenko

50. Boxers, 1914, bronze, 23½ × 18" (cat. 21)
51. Seated Figure, 1913, lithograph, printed in Futurist publication, "Lacerba"
52. Woman (Head on Knee), 1909, bronze, 17" (cat. 3)

51

52

53. *Woman Combing Her Hair,*
1915, bronze, 71" (cat. 26)
54. *Seated Geometric Figure,*
1913, polychromed bronze, 18"
(cat. 16)
55. *Cartoon with Venus, 1911,*
Paris, 1912.

53

54

AU SALON DES INDEPENDANTS 1912
Dessin de G. Léonnec

DEVANT LA VENUS D'ARCHIPENKO

— Vrai? Tu crois que c'est la sœur de celle qui est au Louvre?
Oui, mais elles ne sont pas du même père.

It would be interesting to find the abstract causes responsible for the formations of such styles as Egyptian, Greek, Roman, Gothic and modern. The causes of the creation of the Egyptian style are the Egyptian climate and religious philosophy. Recognizable in this style is also a mysterious calm, a spiritual magnitude and fabulous beauty. This is the consequence of Egypt's religiously profound and refined contact with the universe, with its infinity and eternity. It seems as though the Egyptians wanted to conquer time, and it seems that they succeeded. Egyptian art remains forever an indestructible monument of that great vanished civilization which reached spiritual sublimation. If we compare contemporary Dadaism with Egyptian creative magnitude, Dadaism dwindles to naught.

Archipenko

56

56. Statuette, 1915, bronze, 20⅜" (cat.24)
57. Egyptian Motif, 1917, bronze, 13¾" (cat.33)
58. Standing Figure, 1916, bronze, 12" (cat.27)

57   58

60

59. *Ray, 1919/56, aluminum,*
63¼" (cat. 35)
60. *Der Sturm postcard*
reproducing Archipenko
sculpting Vase Woman, 1919
61. *Left: Vase Woman, 1918,*
bronze, 18"
Right: Vase Woman, 1919,
bronze, 23"
62. *Statue on Triangular Base,*
1914, bronze, 29⅞" (cat. 19)

Cubists, like Futurists and Dadaists and others, want to bring into their circle as many names as possible in order to create a large-scale movement. I find my name used by groups to which I never belonged, for instance Dadaists and Futurists. In reality I am alone and independent.

Archipenko

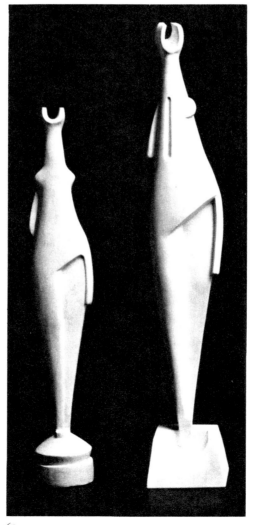

61

62

63

64

63. *Section d'Or de Paris, Galerie La Boëtie, March 1920. Repose and Gondolier on left balcony.*
64. *Archipenko exhibition, Russian pavilion, Venice Biennale, 1920. Penchée, Gondolier, and Head can be seen*
65. *Portuguese, 1916, bronze, 24" (cat.28)*
66. *Geometric Figure with Space and Concave, 1920, bronze, 25½" (cat.37)*

65

It [Section d'Or] consisted of a group of artists working in various styles, not merely Cubism. Our greatest demonstration in Paris was in October, 1912, in a triumphant exhibition at the Hedelbert Gallery and afterwards in the gallery La Boëtie in March, 1920, where I exhibited a large metal construction described by Ivan Goll. In 1914 war disrupted our unity. After the war was over, conflicts began to brew among the group and resulted in the withdrawal of the Dadaists because the painter Survage and I opposed the philosophical concepts of the Dadaists. In 1920 we again resumed our activity. I personally organized the exhibition of Section d'Or in Geneva, Rome and Brussels. Then this historic chapter was closed. Section d'Or was the most beautiful spark of creative energy and solidarity. These men laid the corner-stone of the new era in art. Some of them are gone, some are living, some are immortal.

Archipenko

Berlin, 1921–1923

67

Скульпторъ А. Архипенко

70

68

*67. Masquerade, Berlin, 1919.
Archipenko, with painted hair,
is second from right. Directly
below is Herwarth Walden.
Second woman from left in back row
is Angelica Bruno-Schmitz,
daughter of the German architect
and the future Mrs. Archipenko*
*68. Working on drawing for
lithographic portfolio, Berlin,
circa 1919*
*69. Standing Woman, 1920,
color lithograph, 19⅛ × 12¼",
from the folio "Dreizehn
Steinzeichnungen"*
*70. Caricature by Max Band in
publication, "Spolochy,"
Berlin, 1922*
*71. Reclining, 1922, bronze, 18"
(cat. 42)*

It is difficult to classify an artist into periods.
I never belonged to schools; I was expelled
from schools. I did research, I invented
and experimented, I was then imitated....
Art is one creative flow upward, to
discovery of truths in nature's forms, for
each individual artist, and periods are simply
pigeon-holes in the minds of the critics.

Archipenko

69

74

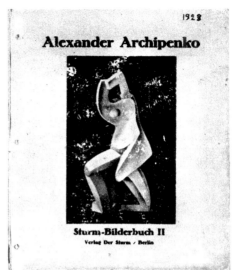

75

76

77

73

72. *Standing Figure, 1920,*
hydrastone, 6 feet. Front and rear
view. Collection of Hessisches
Landesmuseum, Darmstadt
73. *Green Concave, 1913,*
bronze, 19⅛" (cat.17)
74. *"Der Sturm," May 1923.*
Standing Figure on cover
75. *Archipenko monograph*
with introduction by Roland
Schacht, Berlin, 1923.
Green Concave on cover
76. *Berlin, 1918*
77. *Woodcut by Antoine*
Pierre Gallien, Paris, 1918

78

ART MODERNE

TOURNÉE DE L'EXPOSITION
DE
SCULPTURES, SCULPTO-PEINTURES, PEINTURES
DESSINS
DE
ALEXANDRE **ARCHIPENKO**

Préface de Maurice RAYNAL

**Exposition Internationale
d'Art Moderne**
Saison 1920-21.

Exposition d'Œuvres de A. ARCHIPENKO

Expositions en 1921: New-York, Berlin, Dresde
Munich, Duesseldorf, Francfort, Paris.

79

80

*78. Touring retrospective
exhibition, Germany, 1921
79. Catalogue of touring
exhibition, 1921, with preface
by Maurice Raynal
80. With students of his school,
Berlin, 1921
81. Turning Torso, 1921,
bronze, 28" (cat. 38)*

ARCHIPENKO

Published by the
SOCIÉTÉ ANONYME, Inc.
19 East 47th St., New York

82

ARCHIPENKO

TEKST NAPSAL KAREL TEIGE

NÁKL. DEVĚTSILU PRAHA 1923

83

ALEXANDER
ARCHIPENKO

RETROSPEKTIVE
AUSSTELLUNG

ZEICHNUNGEN

AQUARELLE

BILDHAUERWERKE

SCULPTO-PEINTURE

GUSTAV KIEPENHEUER VERLAG
POTSDAM
1921

84

82. *Monograph with appreciation by Ivan Goll, for first one-man exhibition in America, Société Anonyme, New York, 1921*
83. *Retrospective catalogue, Prague, 1923, with introduction by K. Teige*
84. *Retrospective catalogue published in Potsdam, 1921, with text by Ivan Goll*

El pirieta Arcipenko e i ṣo feri de mestier.

85

86

87

85. Caricature, Venice, 1920
86. Monograph with preface by
Lioubomir Mitzitch, Belgrade,
1923
87. Exhibition catalogue with
introduction by Christian Brinton,
Société Anonyme, Kingore
Gallery, New York, 1924,
with Head (cat.40)

HORIZONT
1
ARCHIPENKO

AMATÖR KÖNYVTÁR WIEN

89

ARCHIPENKO

АРХИПЕНКО

DER STURM
MONATSSCHRIFT / HERAUSGEBER: HERWARTH WALDEN
ZWÖLFTER JAHRGANG / DRITTES HEFT

Alexander Archipenko: Sitzende Frau / Zeichnung

88

90

88. *Archipenko monograph,*
"Der Sturm," 1921, with his
drawing, "Sitzende Frau"
on cover
89. *Monograph, Vienna, 1921*
90. *Monograph by Dr. Hans*
Hildebrandt, Berlin, 1923.
Editions in English, French,
German, Spanish, and Ukrainian
91. *Reclining Torso, 1922,*
bronze, 12½ × 21" (cat. 41)

91

92. Declaration for departure
to United States, with
Miss Katherine Dreier
as reference
93. Portrait of Angelica, 1922,
painted wood and plaster, 35"
94. Ukrainian passport with
stamp of Hamburg, port of
departure for America
95. With wife, Angelica,
on board the S.S. Mongolia,
bound for New York,
6 October 1923. Archipenko
is 36 years old

93

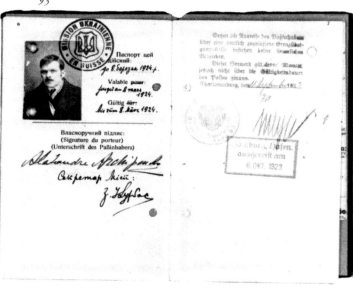

94

ARCHIPENKO, Alexander

(Form No. 228.)

(Established July, 1917, and amended August, 1920.)

2147.

DECLARATION OF ALIEN ABOUT TO DEPART FOR THE UNITED STATES.

Erklärung des nach den Vereinigten Staaten reisenden Ausländers.

(See General Instruction No. 766.)

AMERICAN CONSULATE, **General** **Berlin** **March 16, 23**
Amerikanisches Konsulat, (Place.) (Ort.) (Date.) (Datum.)

I, **Alexander ARCHIPENKO**, a citizen of **Ukraine**
Ich, subject Staatsangehöriger von

bearer of passport No. **1027**, dated **March 8, 1925** issued by **Ukrainian Mission**
Inhaber des Reisepasses No. datiert den ausgestellt durch

Bern

am about to go to the United States of America, accompanied by
bin im Begriff nach den Vereinigten Staaten von Amerika zu reisen, begleitet von

(Names of persons included in declarant's passport, and photographs of whom are attached hereto.)
(Namen der im Reisepass des Erklärenden verzeichneten Personen, deren Lichtbilder darauf geklebt sind.)

I was born **May 30, 1887**, at **Kiev, Russia** 1897
Ich bin geboren am (Date.) (Datum.) (Place.) (Ort.)

My occupation is **sculpter** I last resided at **Berlin, Kurfürstenstr**
Ich bin von Beruf wohnte zuletzt in

126

, for **2** years, and I intend to go to **New York City**
während Monate, have beabsichtige nach (Address in the United States.)
Jahre, (Adresse in den Vereinigten Staaten.)

to remain for **2** years for the purpose of **on business**
zu leben, wo ich Monate, bleiben werde, um (Zweck der Reise.)
Jahre

#10

as shown by letters or affidavits attached hereto, and filed at the Consulate.
wie aus den hier beigefügten bezw. im Konsulate hinterlegten Briefen oder eidlichen Erklärungen erhellt.

I have previously resided in the United States as follows:
Ich habe schon früher in den Vereinigten Staaten gewohnt, wie folgt:

no

(Dates.) (Daten.) (Address.) (Adresse.)

(Object of visit.) (Zweck des Besuches.)

My references are: **Miss Dreier, New York City.**
Meine Referenzen sind (Business address in the United States.) (Geschäftsadresse in den Vereinigten Staaten.)

Geheimrat Justi, Berlin, National Galerie.
(In the consular district where the declaration is made.) (Im Konsularbezirk, wo die Erklärung erfolgt.)

I rendered military service during the World War in the armies of **not**
Ich habe während des Weltkriegs Militärdienst geleistet und zwar in den Heeren von

as follows
wie folgt:

1—928 (OVER.) (UMWENDEN.)

92

RUSSIAN WHO PREDICTS
ART FUTURE FOR U. S.

ALEXANDER ARCHIPENKO.

NOTED SCULPTOR, ARCHIPENKO, HERE

Artist Who Has Just Finished
Bust of Masaryk Hopes to
Found School in N. Y.

CITY'S BEAUTY CAPTIVATES.

Will Give Exhibitions in Large
Cities of United States.

Alexander Archipenko arrived yesterday on the Mongolia, after several weeks at Prague, where he had just finished a bust of President Masaryk of the Czecho-Slovakian Republic. He is considered by many persons the greatest living sculptor, and recently closed a school in Berlin to which students came from all over the world.

He will give exhibitions in the principal cities of the United States this winter, and is desirous of founding in New York "the only modern art school in the world," because, he says, he feels America, which is so fresh and vital and is the only country not jaded and rent by the war, is the place to look for the great art of the future.

While his baggage was being examined, the sculptor looked out the window at the pier sheds and seemed a little disappointed. Then he said:

"Tracks and docks the world over. But when do we get on Broadway?" And as he got to Broadway near the Hotel Astor, where he is staying, he exclaimed: "But it is beautiful! Why doesn't everyone talk of it as a beautiful place?" He was boyishly enthusiastic.

The sculptor is of a little more than medium height, robust, gentle, suave, with a strong Slavic face and the eager eyes of the artist. When asked how long he was going to stay he answered: "Perhaps forever!" He is accompanied by his wife, whose bust he has finished, as he is the museums of Leipsig.

Examples of his work are in nearly all the museums of Europe, and even in Japan. Many collectors in America have examples of his art and some are in Kiev, Russia.

99

Archipenko speaks no English, with the exception of the clearly and perfectly articulated single remark of "I speak no English. My wife will speak for me."

from a newspaper account

TO OPEN SCHOOL FOR SCULPTORS

Archibald Archipenko, Russian sculptor, who comes to America with the intention of opening a school for sculptors in New York city.

Archibald Archipenko, the Russian sculptor who has come to this country primarily to establish a school for sculptors in New York city, is considered by many to be the world's greatest living sculptor. Just before leaving Europe to come to America with his wife, he was engaged in making a bust of President Masaryk of Czecho-Slovakia.

His first question on reaching New York on the Olympic was "When do we get to Broadway?" He does not intend to stop on Broadway immediately, however, as his plans call for exhibitions of his work in many of the principal American cities before he returns here to establish what he proclaims will be "the only modern art school in the world."

Examples of Archipenko's work are in nearly all the museums of Europe as well as in the possession of several American collectors.

Alexander Archipenko, well known Russian sculptor who is working on a bust of Secretary of State Charles E. Hughes, in the Corcoran Art Gallery. The bust will be placed on exhibition next month at his studio in New York.

96. *"The World," New York,*
17 November 1923
97. *New York newspaper,*
autumn, 1923
98. *With his bust of*
U. S. Secretary of State,
Charles E. Hughes,
"Washington Post,"
December 1923
99. *Archipenko with students*
in his first art school in America,
New York, 1923
100. *Diana, 1925, bronze, 23"*
(See front endpaper)
101. *Onward, 1925, bronze,*
21⅞" (cat. 43)
(See front endpaper)

96

97

98

100

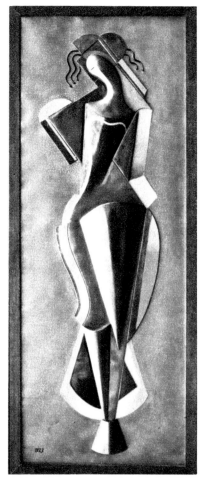

102

*102. Woman, 1923, relief
construction in wood, copper,
brass, new silver, painted, 55",
Collection of Yale University
Art Gallery
103. Standing Concave, 1925,
bronze, 19½" (cat. 45)
104. Saks Fifth Avenue
window decoration in machined
metal, designed by Archipenko,
September 1929. White Torso
(cat. 30) in lower left*

103

America is the only country not jaded
and rent by war. It is the land where
the great art of the future will be
produced. America fires my imagination more than any other country and
embodies more of that flexibility,
that yeastiness, which means life and
vitality and movement.

Archipenko, 1923

Broadway seems to us the most
wonderful street in the world. We had
heard of it long before we came, and
were looking forward most eagerly
to seeing it. In foreign papers one
reads always of Broadway. When we
saw it for the first time at night,
we were like little children who could
do nothing but exclaim over and
over at the many, many lights.

Angelica Archipenko

106

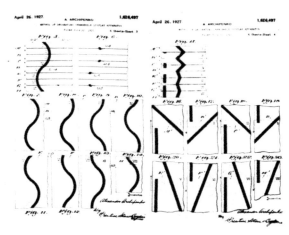

105

Archipentura

Since 1912 in Paris, I have endeavored to record the actual movement in a work of art, and with this object in view I executed the animated construction entitled *Medrano.* These attempts, however, did not bring the desired effect. I again occupied myself with the same idea in 1922 in Berlin. But it was not until 1924 in New York that I succeeded, after numerous technical experiments, in accomplishing my object. I invented a new pictorial method for the execution of real motion on the surface of pictures, and a special apparatus for their demonstration.

Archipentura is a machine, conceived to produce the illusion of the motion of a painted subject, analogous to slow motion in the cinema. I designed, built and patented this machine in 1928 in the United States. Descriptions of this invention appeared in the press, and some of the authors mistakenly used the word "Archipentura" for all my production in art, including sculpture, painting, drawing and prints, without specifying that this name referred exclusively to this machine.

This machine has a box-like shape. Two opposite sides of it are three feet by seven feet. Each of these sides consists of 110 narrow metallic strips, three feet long and one-half inch thick. The strips are installed one on top of another, similar to a Venetian blind. These two sides become the panels for the display of paintings. They are about two feet from each other, and 110 pieces of strong canvas, running horizontally, encircle two oppositely fixed strips. Both ends of the canvases are fastened in the central frame located between two display panels. By mechanically moving the central frame, all 110 canvases simultaneously slide over all the metallic strips, making both panels gradually change their entire surface on which an object is painted. A new portion of specially painted canvas constantly appears. This produces the effect of true motion. A patented method of painting is used to obtain motion. An electrical mechanism in the bottom of the apparatus moves the central frame back and forth, and thousands of consecutive painted fragments appear on the surface to form a total picture. It is not the subject matter, but the changes which become the essence and lie at the origin of this invention.

Archipenko

One-legged ladies that would have delighted old P.T. Barnum; women with arms terminating abruptly at the elbow; hair that looks like potatoes that have begun to sprout or that recalls stringbeans— these are only a few phases of the work of this astounding young Russian sculptor.

The Evening Telegram, New York, 21 October 1923

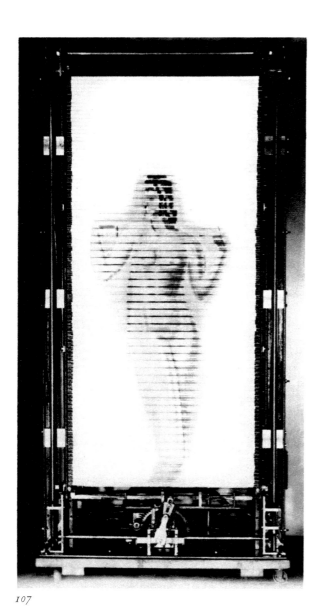

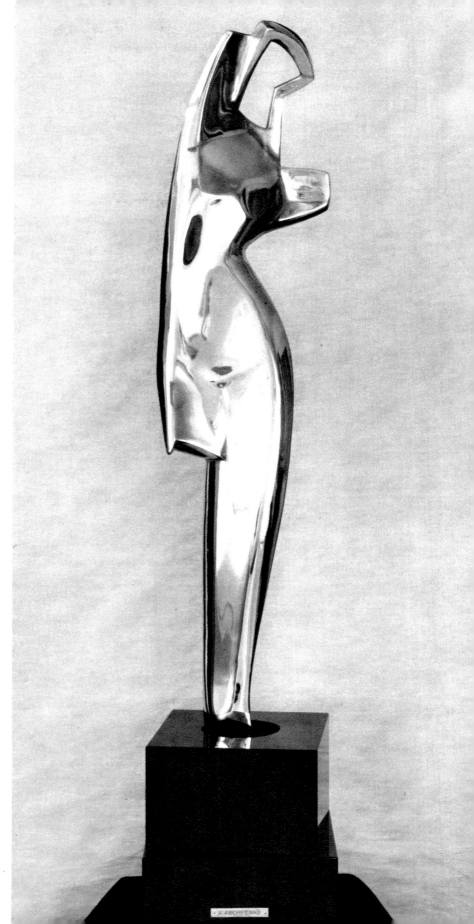

107

105. *Diagram for Archipentura
changeable images*
106. *U.S. Patent for
Archipentura, 26 April 1927*
107. *Archipentura machine, 1924*
108. *Silver Torso, 1931, bronze,
39½" (cat. 46)*

108

109

112

110

111

109. *First car, Woodstock, New York, 1925, where he established art school the same year*
110. *Studio and school, Woodstock, 1932*
111. *Archipenko's cottage which he built at rock quarry, Woodstock, 1929*
112. *Masquerade picnic, Woodstock, 1932. Archipenko on left, Angelica in center*
113. *Angelica, 1925, bronze, gold plated, 12" (cat. 44)*

113

In the last twenty years, natural changes in the methods of art teaching show how quickly the principles of this teaching have become detached from the past. Among the several thousand of my American students, by far the greater proportion are interested in the development of self-expression through art. I have been especially surprised at the strong evidences of a tendency to creative art among the Californians. Last summer, in collaboration with the Chouinard School of Art in Los Angeles, a large group of students produced work rich in imagination, originality, and artistic quality, in a remarkably brief period of time.

Archipenko

116

115

114. Top and bottom:
Torso in Space, 1936, bronze,
5 feet long (cat. 52)
115. Gazing at Oakland
Bay Bridge, 1936
116. With Angelica and
friend, California, 1935

120

117. *Josephine Bonaparte, 1935,*
polychromed bronze, 54"
(cat. 49)
118. *Old Dutch Fisherman,*
1942, bronze, 16" (cat. 55)
119. *Sculpting Madonna in*
California studio, 1936
120. *Madonna, 1936, poly-*
chromed bronze, 24½" (cat. 53)

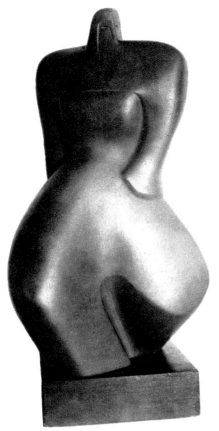

118

119

Creation will lead us out of our difficulties where materialism has failed. Materialism is an attitude which is based on what exists now and what has been; therefore it looks more to the past than to the future. Creation, on the other hand, is primarily a relationship between the individual and experience; therefore, although the past is sometimes called on by the creative mind to help in solving problems, the direction is always towards the future. The psychology of creation vibrates with everything that exists and may possibly exist even in the immaterial realm; therefore creation is never stupidly conservative; it will never retard evolution.

Such is the organization of our civilization that we have not the smallest idea of what creation really means. For instance, in art, a copy of nature cannot be considered a result of creative energy, because purely visual reproduction lacks the necessary individual interpretation.

Where is this [creative] foundation and what is the name of the science that teaches it? Now is the time to establish this science. In its organization, tight collaboration of different branches of science and art is necessary; it cannot be elaborated by one man alone because it needs profound knowledge of many branches of human activity. Physiologists, biologists, artists, philosophers, composers, writers, and inventors, all should be represented by innovators in their fields who have proved by their creativeness that they are not conservative. Above all, it is necessary to keep out commercial interests.

The science of creation should be spread in every country, taught in kindergarten, in all schools and universities. Every man, whoever or wherever he may be, has the ability of creativeness, for this ability is innate in every man. A significant example of the necessity for self-expression through the arts is that now in the United States there are more students of art than ever before. In accord with some law of balance, people are feeling an increasing necessity for spiritual things.

Through my experience—twenty-two years of teaching and thirty years of personal work—I have found that some places are more favorable for creation than others, and it seems to me that California is geographically well suited for the founding of the new science of creation.

Archipenko
from his "The Science of Creation"

81

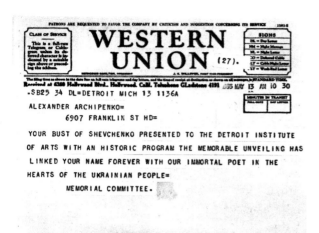

121

121. Telegram from Shevchenko Memorial Committee, 13 May 1935
122. Sculpting portrait of Ukrainian poet, Taras Shevchenko, Chicago, 1935
123. Sculpting Mâ-Meditation in terra cotta, Los Angeles, 1937. Archipenko is 50 years old
124. Modeling the hands of Mâ-Meditation

122

123

Dedication engraved on base of Mâ-Meditation:
Mâ is dedicated to every mother; to everyone who
is in love and suffers from love; to everyone who
creates in the arts and in science; to every hero;
to everyone who is lost in problems; to everyone who
knows and feels Eternity and Infinity.

Archipenko

125

126

127

"The quality of my work cannot be measured by its abstractness as conservatism by its geometrical angularity as curvatures, but only by the large totality of its content and its variety of expression. My old works contain elements of the new and the new contains elements of the old.
By eating only a single apple, one cannot judge the size of the apple tree. History proves that works of art with a truly spiritual content remain immune to criticism."

A. Archipenko

128

125. *Coquette, circa 1950,
color lithograph, 13¾ × 10"
(cat. 91)*
126. *Illuminated Figures,
1948, oil and ink,
22¾ × 16¾"*
127. *Caricature of Archipenko on cover of "Ko Map,"
Lowow, Poland, 1937,
on occasion of his fiftieth
birthday*
128. *Commenting on his work
in his own hand*
129. *Hand print of
Archipenko (actual size)*

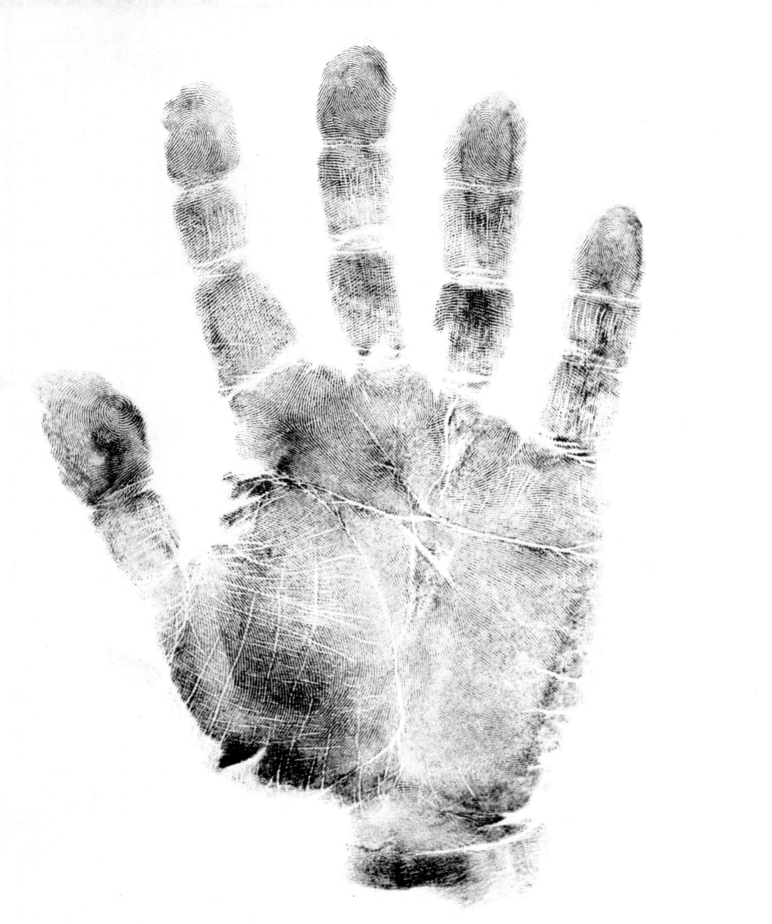

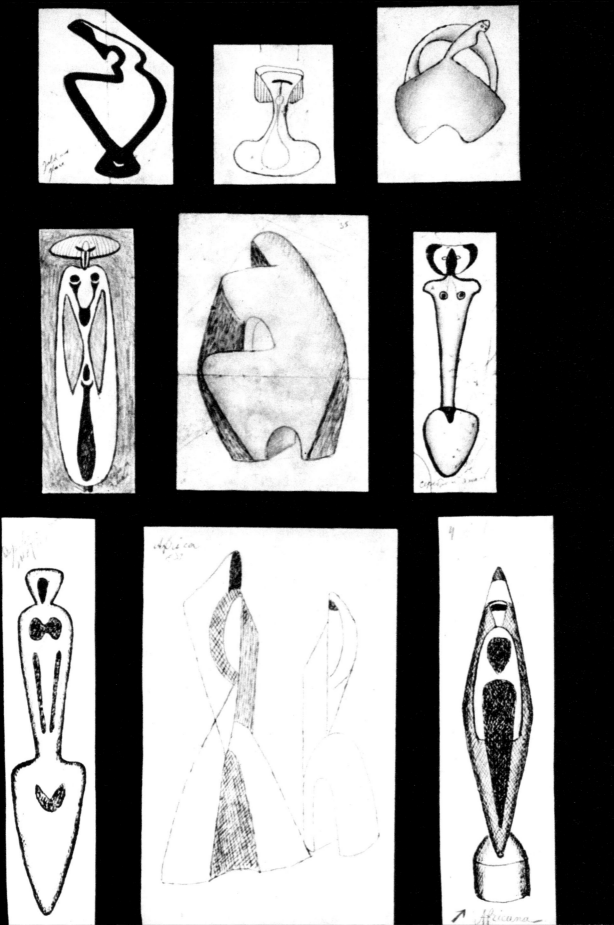

133

131

132

130. *Nine Work Sketches
for Sculpture, 1932–35,
pencil and ink,
27¾ × 16½" (cat. 84)*
131. *Art school's main
building under construction,
Woodstock, July 1940*
132. *Before the party for the
new building*
133. *Construction party*
134. *Beam rises from rock
quarry bed for new art school
building, 1940*

134

135

136

137

138

135. *Summer class,
Woodstock, circa 1950*
136. *Advertisement for summer
and winter art schools*
137. *Carving Onward, 1947,
out of lucite, Woodstock*
138. *In front of completed
main building, Woodstock,
circa 1952*
139. *Lazarus, 1952, bronze,
23" (cat. 57)*

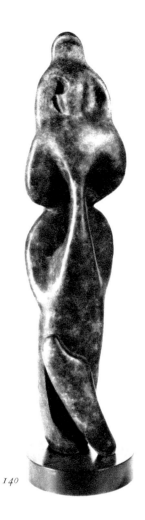

140

141

142

Such usual concepts of sculpture as carving, modeling, casting, cannot be applied to this figure;
nor can the common idea of forming solid volumes be used in this case, because this work consists of new esthetic and spiritual elements which have a relation to modern psychology rather than to the traditional concept of sculpture...
These statues [Iron Figures] are facing east; with the movement of the sun, patterns of bright light and deep shadows produce gradually changing designs. By night, floodlight secreted behind the round base make both figures look like rising phantoms in amber color. On a grey day, the two elongated forms suggest feminine silhouettes decorating the landscape. No other subject matter is to be found in this work but the spirit and expression of rising dignity, purity and beauty of proportions, which are amplified by the play of the light.

Archipenko

*140. Hindu Princess, 1954,
bronze, 53" (cat. 61)
141. Iron Figures,
illuminated at night
142. Teaching at University of
British Columbia, Vancouver,
1956
143. Iron Figure, 1951, 14 feet,
at entrance to University of
Kansas City, in sunlight*

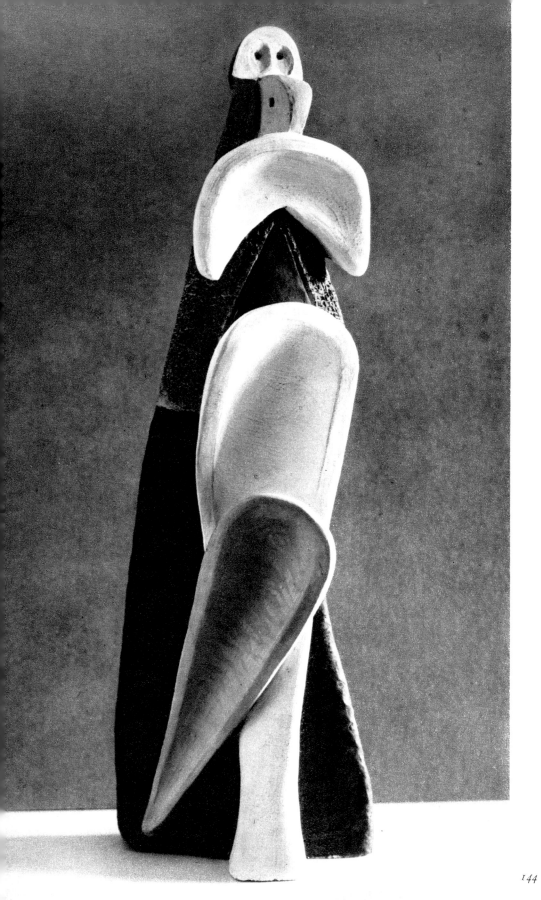

144. *Dualism, 1954,*
polychromed bronze, 22⅜″
(cat. 59)
145. *Scheherazade, 1954,*
polychromed bronze, 12¾″
(cat. 63)

146. *Birth of Venus, 1954,*
bronze, marble, and turquoise, 13"
(cat. 60)
147. *Statue on Aluminum Base,*
1957, polychromed bronze, 18¼"
(cat. 64)

147

148

149

152

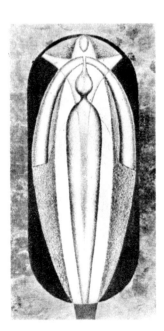

150

151

153

MUSEU DE ARTE MODERNA DE SÃO PAULO

148. *Medieval, 1953, poly-chromed bronze relief,*
25 × 21" (cat. 58)
149. *Retrospective,*
Hessisches Landesmuseum,
Darmstadt, 1955
150. *At gallery reception,*
Caracas, December 1959
151. *Catalogue of drawing*
exhibition, Museu de Arte
Moderna de São Paulo,
November 1952. Offenbarung,
1952, on cover
152. *Opening of Archipenko*
exhibition, Saarland Museum,
Saarbrücken, 1960
153. *Woman with Hat, 1954,*
bronze, 14½" (cat. 62)

154

155

154. Sculpting Dignity in
New York studio, 1960
155. Building up the clay on
Tapering Figure (cat. 71)
in Woodstock, 1960
156. Dignity, 1961, poly-
chromed bronze, 33½″ (cat. 70)
157. Queen of Sheba, 1961,
polychromed bronze, 65″
(cat. 74)

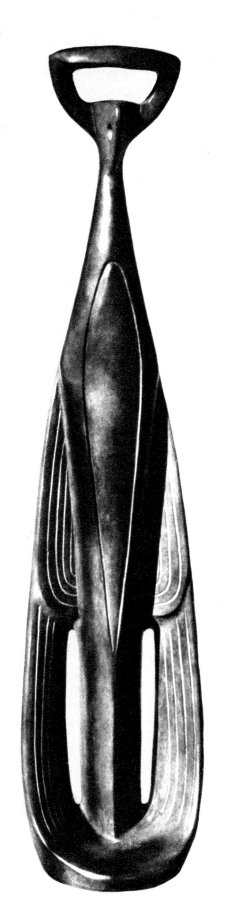

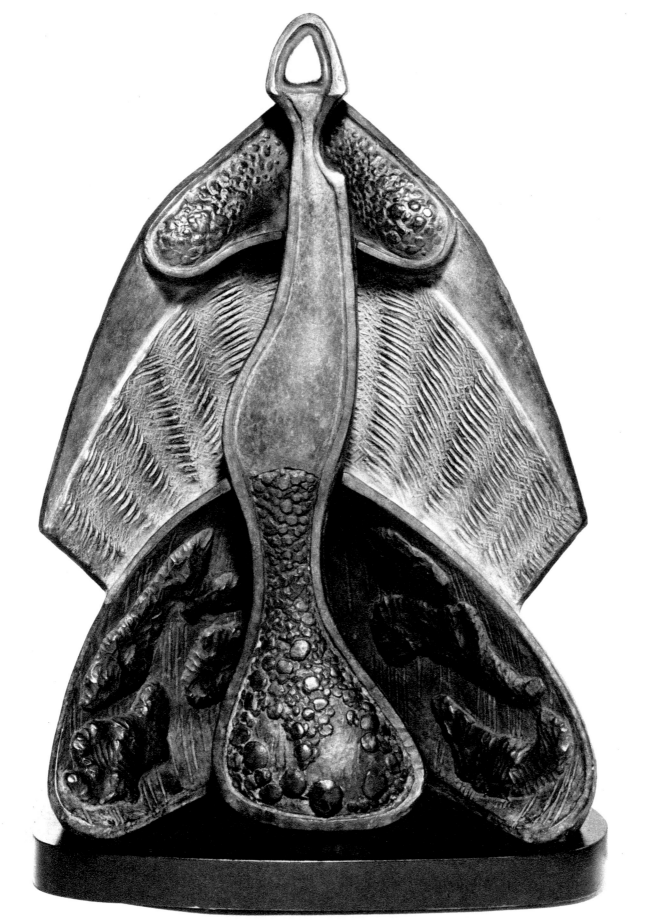

159   *160*   *161*

JUNGE KUNST BAND 40
ALEXANDER ARCHIPENKO
VON ERICH WIESE

NATIONAL·INSTITUTE
OF·ARTS·AND·LETTERS
IN·RECOGNITION·OF·DISTINGUISHED·WORK·IN·THE·ARTS
ALEXANDER ARCHIPENKO
WAS·ELECTED·TO·MEMBERSHIP·AT·THE·ANNUAL
MEETING·HELD·IN·THE·CITY·OF·NEW·YORK · 1962

SECRETARY

PRESIDENT

162

*158. Festive, 1961, polychromed
bronze, 26½" (cat.75)*
*159. Monograph by Erich Wiese,
Leipzig, 1923*
*160. Archipenko with second wife,
Frances, reunited with Professor
Wiese, Darmstadt, 1960*
*161. With Frances,
Saarland Museum, 1960*
*162. Membership in National
Institute of Arts and Letters,
New York, 1962*

*163. Walking Torso, 1963,
bronze, 14" (cat.76)
164. Italian caricatures of
Archipenko's work at the
Venice Biennale, 1920
165. With Mayor of Rome at
historical section of Ente Premi
Roma exhibition, 1963.
Archipenko is 75 years old
166. Title page of retrospective
catalogue at Ente Premi Roma,
1963
167. Islander, 1958, polychromed
bronze, 22" (cat.68)
168. Who is She?, 1957, polychromed bronze, 11½" (cat.67)*

163

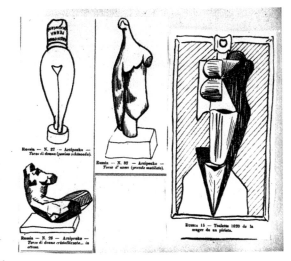

164

165

ALEXANDER ARCHIPENKO

scritti di

GIOVANNI SANGIORGI
GINO SEVERINI
ALEXANDER ARCHIPENKO

testimonianze di

GUILLAUME APOLLINAIRE
BLAISE CENDRARS
THÉODOR DAUBLER
HERWARTH WALDEN
ARDENGO SOFFICI
IVAN GOLL
MOHOLY - NAGY
ULRICH GERTZ
PIERRE GUEGNEN
GIEDION WELCHEN
MICHEL SEUPHOR
HANS FUCHS

ENTE PREMI ROMA
1963

166

168

103

169. *Helping Frances with her first lithograph, Erker-Presse, St. Gallen, Switzerland, 1963*
170. *Poster for retrospective, Galerie "Im Erker," St. Gallen, 1962–63*
171. *Luminosité des Formes, 1963, lithograph, from portfolio printed in St. Gallen, 30 × 22"* (cat. 102)
172. *With his dalmatian, Sappho, New York, 1963*
173. *Woman in the Chair, 1963, polychromed bronze, 11⅝"* (cat. 77)

169

ARCHIPENKO
17. November 1962 – 10. Januar 1963 GALERIE »IM ERKER«
am Gallusplatz St. Gallen

170

171

172

174. *Last photograph*
of the sculptor, in his
New York studio, 1963,
completing King Solomon,
his only sculpture designed
for monumental scale
up to 60 feet.
175. *King Solomon, 1963,*
bronze, 26¼"
176. *King Solomon, 1963,*
bronze, 67" (cat.78)

175

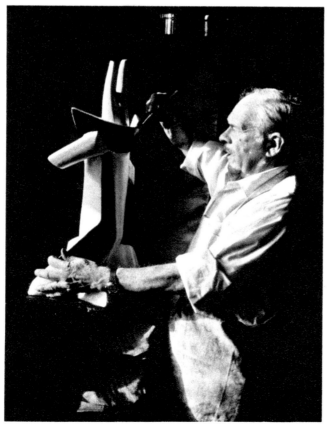

174

177

178

177. *Completed façade of main building, Woodstock, 1968. Mrs. Archipenko on balcony*
178. *Interior of main school building, Woodstock, 1968, now the home of Frances Archipenko*

The Archipenko Collection and Archive

The Archipenko archive consists of over twenty thousand single items of correspondence, notations, manuscripts, catalogues, clippings and sculpture and personal photographs conserved by my husband throughout his lifetime, despite the handicap of travel, relocation and storage. He was naturally an archivist as well as collector and it was more a respect for and pursuit of historical objectivity in the arts and what he called "the science of creativity," rather than nostalgia, that led him to amass such a voluminous record of his life and works. The contents of this book are comprised entirely of material from this archive and give some indication of the scope of the record that has been left behind. Realizing the importance of this archive, I have taken steps towards its permanent preservation, being concerned with proper access to its contents and the inevitable deterioration of paper. With the cooperation of the Archives of American Art, the entire archive has been microfilmed and is available for scholarly research in Detroit, New York and Washington, D.C. Photographic prints from over one hundred of these microfilm frames form an archive section which supplements the Archipenko Retrospective tour of European nations and provide many of the illustrations in this publication. Preservation for historical and esthetic purposes is also being undertaken with respect to many of my husband's works and the Woodstock atelier itself. A group of his sculptures, paintings, drawings and prints in my collection will remain intact for research and general viewing as circumstances permit. In addition, the former main school building at Woodstock, designed and built by my husband during a period of hardship, and a symbol of his life's teachings, will also be preserved in the woodland and rock setting which he loved so much.

Frances Archipenko
Woodstock, New York

Biographical Chronology

1887

May 30. Born in Kiev, Ukraine, Russia, to Porfiry Antonovich and Poroskovia Wassilievna Machova Archipenko. Paternal grandfather, icon painter. Father, mechanical engineer and inventor, professor of engineering, University of Kiev.
Privately tutored to age nine, when entered Kiev Gymnasium.

1900

Injured leg bone in bicycle accident. Confined to bed age 13–14. Studied and copied Michelangelo drawings from book given to him by grandfather.

1902

Having grasped the relationship between mathematics and art, decided on career in art. Inspired by "the fact that Leonardo's creative genius not only covered art, but science as well as engineering and that he considered mathematics as the foundation of all arts."
Entered art school in Kiev to study painting and then sculpture. Influenced by Byzantine tradition in art, the writings of Adreyev, and later, the revolution of 1905.

1905

Expelled from art school because he criticized his teachers for being "too old-fashioned and academic."

1906

First one-man show in a town in the Ukraine.
Went to Moscow, worked and participated in different group shows.

1908

Left for Paris at age 20.
Entered Ecole des Beaux Arts, but left after two weeks, finding the academic system too confining and tedious.
Continued study of art independently in museums. "My real school was the Louvre and I attended it daily." Inspired especially by Egyptian, Assyrian, archaic Greek, and early Gothic works.
Established Montparnasse studio where Modigliani, Gaudier-Brzeska and others studied sculpture with him.

1909

Produced series of revolutionary sculptures, such as *Seated Black Torso, Suzanne,* and *Woman (Head on Knee).*

1910

Began exhibiting in Salon des Artistes Indépendants (showed in 1910, 1911, 1912, 1913, 1914).

1911

Exhibited in Salon d'Automne, Paris (also in 1912, 1913, 1919). French newspaper caricatured sculpture, *Woman with Cat,* which was displayed in this exhibition.

1912

Opened own art school in Paris.
Section d'Or formed in Paris. Archipenko among its members, who exhibited together until 1914 and again for a short time after the war. Included Picasso, Braque, Gris, Léger, Delaunay, de La Fresnaye, Villon, Picabia, and Marcel Duchamp.
First one-man exhibition in Germany at Folkwang Museum, Hagen. Catalogue analysis by Guillaume Apollinaire.
Produced sculpture, *Medrano I (Juggler),* the first three-dimensional construction in modern sculpture in various painted materials (wood, glass, metal wire). Rejected by jury of Salon d'Automne in Paris; exhibited in Budapest, 1913, in Exposition d'Art Moderne, organized by Alexandre Mercereau.
Started creating reliefs, generally made of plaster, carve d painted, which he named "Sculpto-Peintures." These are the first sculpto-paintings in modern art.
Created *Walking Woman,* first modern sculpture for bstracted concaves to create implied volume and abstracted voids (openings through mass).

Produced *Dance,* one of first examples in modern sculpture of creating a spatial environment; reproduced and ridiculed on the cover of the English magazine, *The Sketch,* of 29 October 1913.

1913
Represented by four sculptures and five drawings in Armory Show in New York, including *Family Life* which was ridiculed by caricature in *The World* (New York).
First one-man exhibition at Der Sturm Gallery, Berlin.
Produced highly polychromed sculpture, *Carrousel Pierrot.*
Created *Head,* construction with crossing planes.

1914
Created *Boxers,* one of the most abstract modern sculptures done to that date.
Produced *Gondolier,* caricatured in *Le Bonnet Rouge,* No. 16, 7 March 1914 (Paris).
Cubist exhibition held by Mánes Society, Prague, organized by Alexandre Mercereau, included five sculptures of Archipenko, five of Brancusi, and six of Duchamp-Villon.

1915
Produced sculpture, *Woman Combing Her Hair,* which again used deep concaves and void.

1914–1918
Spent war years working on his sculpture in a villa at Cimiez, a suburb of Nice, loaned him by a wealthy friend.

1918
Produced sculpture, *Ray,* first of three highly simplified vase figures.
Left collection of plasters of early work with Monsieur and Madame Jean Verdier in Cannes, for safe-keeping, on the eve of his departure for Germany.

1919
Began extensive tour exhibiting his works in various European cities, including Geneva, Zurich, Paris, London, Brussels, Athens, Berlin, Munich, etc., lasting through 1921.

1920
Large one-man show in Biennale Exhibition, Venice (XIIª Esposizione Internazionale d'Arte). Ridiculed in *Telegrafo Livorno* of 11 June 1920. Cardinal La Fontaine, Patriarch of Venice, advised the faithful not to attend.
Section d'Or, of which Archipenko was member, resumed exhibiting after war (in Paris at Galerie Weill, and in Brussels, 1920; in Rome—organized by Enrico Prampolini, and in Geneva, 1921).

1921
Married Angelica Bruno-Schmitz, German sculptress and great granddaughter of artist, Bonaventura Genelli.
Moved to Berlin, opened own art school.
First one-man exhibition in United States at Société Anonyme, Museum of Modern Art, New York City. Monograph, *Archipenko,* by Ivan Goll (Société Anonyme, 1921) published in connection with this exhibition.
Symposium on the *Psychology of Modern Art and Archipenko* held at Société Anonyme, New York.
Retrospective exhibition in Potsdam. Catalogue introduction by Ivan Goll.
Archipenko Album by Ivan Goll, Theodor Däubler and Blaise Cendrars published in Potsdam by Gustav Kiepenheuer Verlag.
One-man exhibition at Der Sturm Gallery, Berlin.

1923
Moved to the United States. Arrived in New York by liner, S.S. *Mongolia.* Opened art school in New York City.
Professor Hans Hildebrandt's monograph, *Alexander Archipenko,* published in Berlin by Ukrainske Slowo in English, French, German, and Ukrainian (in Spanish by Editora Internacional, Buenos Aires).
Roland Schacht's "Alexander Archipenko," *Sturm Bilderbuch II,* published in Berlin by Verlag Der Sturm.
Professor Erich Wiese's article, "Alexander Archipenko," *Junge Kunst,* Vol. 40, published in Leipzig by Verlag von Klinkhardt und Biermann.

1924
Opened summer art school in Woodstock, New York.
Invented variable image system as "movable painting" known as "Peinture Changeante" (also called "Archipentura"), (U.S. Patent 1,626,496 granted in 1927), dedicated to Thomas Edison and Albert Einstein. "The observer is shown a screen on which is painted an abstract form. Archipenko presses an electric button, the abstract form begins to change proceeding through most of the phases of the female body Archipenko painted and chiseled." Featured at one-man exhibition at The Anderson Galleries, New York, in 1928.

1927
One-man exhibition, Société des Artistes Nikwa, Tokyo, Japan.

1928
Became an American citizen.

1929
Number of exhibitions of works of students at Arko, a laboratory school for ceramics which Archipenko established in New York City.
Purchased thirteen acres on abandoned rock quarry site near Woodstock, New York, art colony. Began construction of what was to be a complex of art school buildings, his own studio, and new location for his summer art school.

1932
Started to lecture on theories of creativeness in colleges and universities on Pacific Coast, in the Middle West and the East.

1933
Taught at Mills College, Oakland, California (summer session), and at Chouinard School, Los Angeles.

1935
Took up residence in California, opened own art school in Los Angeles, and exhibited in several western cities.

1935–1936
Taught summer sessions, University of Washington, Seattle.

1937
Moved to Chicago; opened school of creative fine arts.
Associate instructor at New Bauhaus School of Industrial Arts, Chicago.

1939
Created *Moses,* seven-foot-high sculpture, for benefit of artists exiled by Fascist regimes of Europe, but its planned tour was cancelled owing to delays of wartime transportation. During the Nazi purge of "decadent modern art," twenty-two of his paintings and most of his sculpture then owned by German museums were confiscated; and his work was singled out for attack in the Nazi book, *Säuberung des Kunsttempels,* by Wolfgang Willrich (Munich: J. F. Lehmanns, 1937).
Returned to New York. Re-opened art school as well as summer school in Woodstock, New York.

1944
Taught at the Dalton School, New York.

1946
Taught at the Institute of Design, Chicago.

1947
Produced *Seated Figure,* the first carved plastic sculpture illuminated from within, featured at his 78th one-man show at the New York Galleries of the Associated American Artists, in 1948.

1950
Taught at the University of Kansas City, Kansas City, Missouri. Commissioned to create two statues for the entrance of the University. The two identical *Iron Figures,* 14-foot-high constructions with crossing planes, were completed in 1951.

1950–1951
Made lecture tour of southern cities of United States.

1951
Taught at Carmel Institute of Art, Carmel, California; at the University of Oregon, Eugene, Oregon; and at the University of Washington, Seattle.

1952
Taught at University of Delaware, Newark, Delaware.
Delegate to UNESCO, New York City.
One-man exhibition, Museum of Modern Art, São Paulo, Brazil.

1953
Inaugurated Associate Member of International Institute of Arts and Letters.
One-man exhibition, El Instituto Guatemalteco-Americano, Guatemala City, Guatemala.

1955–1956
Tour of one-man exhibition to six German cities.

1955

Began work on book, *Archipenko: Fifty Creative Years 1908–1958*, a 346-page book which includes a 52-page manifesto on creativity by Archipenko, an extensive bibliography, quotations, and 292 plates of his works.

1956

Taught at the University of British Columbia, Vancouver, Canada.
Produced *Revolving Figure (The Art of Reflection)*, a 78-inch-high, motorized, revolving construction with crossing planes, made of wood, mother-of-pearl, formica, and metal.

1957

Created *Cleopatra*, a 38-inch by 84-inch sculpto-painting of wood and bakelite, polychromed.
First one-man show at Perls Galleries, New York.
December 5. Angelica died at age 65.

1959

Awarded Medaglia D'Oro at XIIIª Biennale d'Arte Triveneta, IIIº Concorso Internazionale del Bronzetto, Sala della Ragione, Padua, Italy, in October.

1960

Book, *Archipenko: Fifty Creative Years 1908–1958*, by Alexander Archipenko published by Tekhne Publications, established by Archipenko for the purpose of publishing this book.
August 1. Married Frances Gray, a sculptor and former student.
Recovery of plasters of early works stored in 1918 by Monsieur and Madame Jean Verdier in a gardener's cottage on their property in Cannes.

1961

Produced 66-inch-high sculpture, *Queen of Sheba*, his last large bronze.

1962

Elected to the Department of Art of the National Institute of Arts and Letters.

1963

Produced *Les Formes Vivantes*, a series of ten lithographs, his last graphics, at Erker-Presse in St. Gallen, Switzerland.
Large retrospective exhibition of Archipenko sculpture, drawings and prints at Ente Premi Roma in Rome and Centro Culturale S. Fedele in Milan in 1963, and at Galerie Stangl in Munich in 1964.

1964

February 25. Alexander Archipenko died in New York, shortly after casting his last sculpture, *King Solomon*.

1967–1969

Retrospective, "Alexander Archipenko: A Memorial Exhibition," organized by the UCLA Art Galleries, shown at ten museums across the country: Cincinnati Art Museum; Colorado Springs Fine Arts Center; Dallas Museum of Fine Arts; Fine Arts Gallery of San Diego; Munson-Williams-Proctor Institute; National Collection of Fine Arts, Smithsonian Institution; Phoenix Art Museum; The UCLA Art Galleries; Walker Art Center; Washington University, St. Louis.

List of Works

All sculptures are in bronze, unless otherwise indicated. Height precedes width; a single dimension refers to height.

1. *Adam and Eve,* 1908, 19¾'' (Plate 8)
2. *Crossed Arms,* 1908, 13⅛''
3. *Woman (Head on Knee),* 1909, 17'' (Plate 52)
4. *Black Seated Torso,* 1909, 15'' (Plate 9)
5. *Mother and Child,* 1910, 13¾'' (Plate 20)
6. *Woman with Cat,* 1910, 13¼'' (Plate 14)
7. *Repose,* 1911, 13½ × 14½'' (Plate 30)
8. *Draped Woman,* 1911, 22'' (Plate 19)
9. *Madonna of the Rocks,* 1912, 20¼'' (Plate 21)
10. *Family Life,* 1912, 22'' (Plate 35)
11. *Walking,* 1912, 52½'' (Plate 42)
12. *Dance,* 1912, 24⅛'' (Plate 22)
13. *Seated Figure,* 1912, 15½'' (Plate 29)
14. *Blue Dancer,* 1913, 41'' (Plate 27)
15. *Head,* 1913, 14⅞'' (Plate 38)
16. *Seated Geometric Figure,* 1913, 18'' (Plate 54)
17. *Green Concave,* 1913, 19⅛'' (Plate 73)
18. *Small Reclining Figure,* 1913, 4⅛ × 12⅛''
19. *Statue on Triangular Base,* 1914, 29⅞'' (Plate 62)
20. *Gondolier,* 1914, 64'' (Plate 47)
21. *Boxers,* 1914, 23½ × 18'' (Plate 50)
22. *Woman with Fan,* 1914, 35¾'' (Plate 43)
23. *Geometric Statuette,* 1914, 27''
24. *Statuette,* 1915, 20⅜'' (Plate 56)
25. *Seated Woman Combing Her Hair,* 1915, 21⅛''
26. *Woman Combing Her Hair,* 1915, 71'' (Plate 53)
27. *Standing Figure,* 1916, 12'' (Plate 58)
28. *Portuguese,* 1916, 24'' (Plate 65)
29. *Seated Black Concave,* 1916, 30½''
30. *White Torso,* 1916, 18¾'' (Plate 104)
31. *Española,* 1916, 21 × 23'' (Plate 45)
32. *Walking Soldier,* 1917, 46'' (Plate 46)
33. *Egyptian Motif,* 1917, 13¾'' (Plate 57)
34. *Still Life with Book and Vase on the Table,* 1918, 13¾ × 18'' (Plate 44)
35. *Ray,* 1919/56, aluminum, 63¼'' (Plate 59)
36. *Standing Woman,* 1920, 28½ × 16⅜'' (front cover)
37. *Geometric Figure with Space and Concave,* 1920, 25½'' (Plate 66)
38. *Turning Torso,* 1921, 28'' (Plate 81)
39. *Symmetrical Torso,* 1921, 28½''
40. *Head,* 1922, 15½'' (Plate 87)
41. *Reclining Torso,* 1922, 12½ × 21'' (Plate 91)
42. *Reclining,* 1922, 18'' (Plate 71)
43. *Onward,* 1925, 21⅞'' (Plate 101)
44. *Angelica,* 1925, 12'' (Plate 113)
45. *Standing Concave,* 1925, 19½'' (Plate 103)
46. *Silver Torso,* 1931, 39½'' (Plate 108)
47. *Mâ-Meditation,* 1932, 30½'' (Sketch for *Mâ-Meditation,* 1937, 5 feet)
48. *Family Life,* 1935, 18 × 31'' (Plate 33)
49. *Josephine Bonaparte,* 1935, 54'' (Plate 117)

50. *Seated, Black,* 1936, 21⅛"
51. *Fiancée,* 1936, 19"
52. *Torso in Space,* 1936, 5 feet long (Plate 114)
53. *Madonna,* 1936, 24½" (Plate 120)
54. *Hollywood Torso,* 1936, 28"
55. *Old Dutch Fisherman,* 1942, 16" (Plate 118)
56. *Seated Figure,* 1947, 37"
57. *Lazarus,* 1952, 23" (Plate 139)
58. *Medieval,* 1953, 25×21" (Plate 148)
59. *Dualism,* 1954, 22⅜" (Plate 144)
60. *Birth of Venus,* 1954, 13" (Plate 146)
61. *Hindu Princess,* 1954, 53" (Plate 140)
62. *Woman with Hat,* 1954, 14½" (Plate 153)
63. *Scheherazade,* 1954, 12¾" (Plate 145)
64. *Statue on Aluminum Base,* 1957, 18¼" (Plate 147)
65. *Objects on the Table,* 1957, 25×16¾"
66. *Flying,* 1957, 11½"
67. *Who is She?,* 1957, 11½" (Plate 168)
68. *Islander,* 1958, 22" (Plate 167)
69. *Statuette,* 1959, 15"
70. *Dignity,* 1961, 33½" (Plate 156)
71. *Tapering Figure,* 1961, 29½" (Plate 155)
72. *Kimono,* 1961, 31½" (back cover)
73. *Linear Oriental,* 1961, 24½"
74. *Queen of Sheba,* 1961, 65" (Plate 157)
75. *Festive,* 1961, 26½" (Plate 158)
76. *Walking Torso,* 1963, 14" (Plate 163)
77. *Woman in the Chair,* 1963, 11⅝" (Plate 173)
78. *King Solomon,* 1963, 67" (including bronze base) (Plate 176)

Drawings

79. *Nine Work Sketches for Sculpture,* 1932–1935, pencil, 29¼×18⅝"
80. *Nine Work Sketches for Sculpture,* 1932–1935, pencil, 29½×18¾"
81. *Five Work Sketches for Sculpture,* 1932–1935, pencil, 26¾×19⅜"
82. *Ten Work Sketches for Sculpture,* 1932–1935, pencil, 28½×17¾"
83. *Ten Work Sketches for Sculpture,* 1932–1935, pencil 26¾×21"
84. *Nine Work Sketches for Sculpture,* 1932–1935, pencil and ink, 27¾×16½" (Plate 130)

Prints

85. *Bending,* 1920, etching, 9¾×5⅞"
86. *Kneeling,* 1920, etching, 7×5"
87. *Figure Study,* 1920, lithograph, 19⅛×12¼". From the portfolio, "Dreizehn Steinzeichnungen"
88. *Still Life with Vase,* 1920, lithograph, 17⅛×9½". From the portfolio, "Dreizehn Steinzeichnungen"
89. *Angelica,* 1922, etching, 6½×4¼"
90. *Woman,* 1922, lithograph, 15½×9½". From the portfolio, "Die Schaffenden"
91. *Coquette,* circa 1950, lithograph, 13¾×10" (Plate 125)
92. *Bathers,* circa 1950, lithograph, 13×8½"
93. *Torso in Space,* 1953, lithograph, serigraphy, and embossing, 14⅞×23¾"
94. Lithographic poster for retrospective, Galerie "Im Erker," St. Gallen, 1962–1963, proof before letters, 35×22" (see Plate 170)
95. *Les Amoureux,* 1963, lithograph, 30×22". From the portfolio, "Les Formes Vivantes"
96. *La Danse Noire,* 1963, lithograph, 30×22". From the portfolio, "Les Formes Vivantes"
97. *Le Groupe,* 1963, lithograph, 30×22". From the portfolio, "Les Formes Vivantes" (Frontispiece)
98. *Les Mannequins,* 1963, lithograph, 30×22". From the portfolio, "Les Formes Vivantes"
99. *La Famille d'une Forme,* 1963, lithograph, 30×22". From the portfolio, "Les Formes Vivantes"
100. *Le Couronnement des Formes,* 1963, lithograph, 30×22". From the portfolio, "Les Formes Vivantes"
101. *Les Formes Encerclées,* 1963, lithograph, 22×30". From the portfolio, "Les Formes Vivantes"
102. *Luminosité des Formes,* 1963, lithograph, 30×22". From the portfolio, "Les Formes Vivantes" (Plate 171)
103. *Les Formes Majestueuses,* 1963, lithograph, 30×22". From the portfolio, "Les Formes Vivantes"
104. *Les Rendez-vous des Quatre Formes,* 1963, lithograph, 30×22". From the portfolio, "Les Formes Vivantes"

Selective Bibliography

Archipenko, Alexander, *Archipenko: Fifty Creative Years 1908–1958,* New York, Tekhne (245 West 19th Street, New York, N.Y. 10011), 1960.

Goll, Ivan, "Archipenko," *Horizont,* Vienna, 1921.

Goll, Ivan, *Archipenko: An Appreciation,* translated by Mary Knoblauch, New York, Société Anonyme, Inc. (1921).

Goll, Ivan, Theodor Däubler and Blaise Cendrars, *Archipenko Album,* Potsdam, Gustav Kiepenheuer Verlag, 1921.

Golubetz, Nicola, *Archipenko,* Lwow, Ukrainske Mistetstvo, 1922.

Fezzi, Elda, "Aleksandr Archipenko," *I Maestri della Scultura,* 44, Milano, Fratelli Fabbri Editori, 1966.

Hildebrandt, Professor Hans, *Alexander Archipenko,* Berlin, Ukrainske Slowo, 1923.
   (Edition appeared in four languages: English, French, German, Ukrainian.)

Hildebrandt, Professor Hans, *Alejandro Archipenko,* Buenos Aires, Editora Internacional, 1923. (Spanish edition.)

Karshan, Donald H., *Archipenko: Content and Continuity 1908–1963,* Chicago, Kovler Gallery: Chicago, 1968.

Mitzitch, Lioubomir, editor, *Archipenko, Plastique Nouvelle,* Belgrade, Editions Zenit, 1923.

Raynal, Maurice, *A. Archipenko,* Rome, "Valori Plastici," 1923.

Sangiorgi, Giovanni and Gino Severini, *Alexander Archipenko,* Rome, Ente Premi Roma, 1963.

Schacht, Dr. Roland, *Alexander Archipenko, Sturm-Bilderbuch II,* Berlin, Der Sturm Verlag, 1923.

Wiese, Professor Erich, "Alexander Archipenko," *Junge Kunst,* Vol. 40, Leipzig, Verlag von Klinkhardt und Biermann, 1923.

Wight, Frederick S., Katharine Kuh and Donald H. Karshan, *Alexander Archipenko: A Memorial Exhibition 1967–1969,* Los Angeles, University of California at Los Angeles, 1967.

This book was set in Monotype Universe and Garamond by Conzett & Huber of Zurich, Switzerland, and printed in monogravure and offset by Amilcare Pizzi, S.p.A. of Milan, Italy

Design by Ulrich Ruchti, assisted by Ellen Hsiao

Photograph on p. 25 by Hershel Womack; installation shown was designed by Harry Lowe, Curator of Exhibits
Photograph on p. 106 (Plate 174) by Andrew Paschuk, New York
Photographs on p. 108 by The Tom Reynolds Studio

Back endpaper: Archipenko with students, Woodstock, New York, circa 1950